HEALTHY RECIPES FOR TWO SENIORS

"Cookbook for Two Seniors" is a culinary treasure designed especially for seniors who are looking for simple, yet delicious recipes.

This cookbook features a wide range of dishes, including breakfasts, soups, stews, main dishes, side dishes, salads, snacks, and desserts, all of which have been carefully curated to cater to the unique needs and tastes of seniors.

With easy-to-follow instructions, step-by-step guides, and helpful tips, this cookbook is the perfect kitchen companion for seniors who love to cook for themselves or for two.

Cookbook
for Two Seniors
Healthy Recipes

HEALTHY RECIPES PERFECTLY PORTIONED FOR TWO SENIORS

JULIA T. HICKS

COOKBOOK FOR TWO SENIORS
Healthy Recipes Perfectly Portioned for Two Seniors.

© Cookbooks for Two Seniors
© Julia T. Hicks
© E.G.P. Editorial

Printed in USA.
ISBN-13: 9798391447771

THE IMPORTANCE OF NUTRITION FOR SENIORS

As people age, their nutritional needs change, and maintaining a well-balanced diet becomes increasingly important for overall health and well-being. Good nutrition plays a vital role in supporting seniors' physical and mental health, helping them maintain their independence, and reducing the risk of developing various age-related health issues. Here are some key reasons why nutrition is particularly important for seniors:

- Promotes healthy aging: A nutrient-rich diet can help seniors maintain muscle strength, bone density, and overall body function, which are essential components of healthy aging. Eating a balanced diet with a variety of fruits, vegetables, whole grains, lean proteins, and healthy fats can provide seniors with the nutrients they need for optimal health.

- Supports the immune system: As we age, our immune system becomes less efficient, making seniors more susceptible to infections and illnesses. A nutritious diet can help support the immune system by providing essential vitamins, minerals, and antioxidants. These nutrients can help protect seniors from illness and improve their recovery when they do get sick.

- Prevents and manages chronic diseases: Many chronic diseases prevalent among seniors, such as diabetes, heart disease, and osteoporosis, can be prevented or managed through proper nutrition. A diet rich in fruits, vegetables, whole grains, and lean proteins can help regulate blood sugar levels, reduce inflammation, and promote heart health. Additionally, consuming adequate amounts of calcium and vitamin D can help maintain bone density and prevent osteoporosis.

- Supports mental health and cognitive function: A well-balanced diet is not only essential for physical health but also plays a crucial role in maintaining mental health and cognitive function in seniors. Nutrients like omega-3 fatty acids, vitamin B12, and antioxidants found in fruits and vegetables can help support brain health, prevent cognitive decline, and reduce the risk of developing dementia and Alzheimer's disease.

- Enhances energy levels and mood: Consuming a balanced diet with the right combination of nutrients can help seniors maintain their energy levels and support overall mood. Eating regular meals with adequate amounts of complex carbohydrates, proteins, and healthy fats can help stabilize blood sugar levels, prevent energy crashes, and promote a sense of well-being.

- Maintains healthy weight and digestion: Proper nutrition is essential for maintaining a healthy weight and supporting digestive health in seniors. Consuming fiber-rich foods like whole grains, fruits, and vegetables can help prevent constipation and promote regular bowel movements. Additionally, a well-balanced diet can help seniors maintain a healthy weight, reducing the risk of obesity-related health issues.

- Encourages social interaction: Sharing meals with family, friends, or neighbors can provide seniors with valuable opportunities for social interaction and emotional support. Eating together can help foster a sense of community and belonging, which is essential for mental and emotional well-being.

In conclusion, good nutrition is crucial for seniors to maintain their overall health, prevent and manage chronic diseases, support cognitive function, and enhance their quality of life.

Providing seniors with access to nutritious meals and promoting a well-balanced diet can help them age gracefully and live independently for as long as possible.

TABLE OF CONTENTS

BREAKFASTS

OATMEAL WITH FRESH FRUIT AND NUTS

Ingredients:

- 1 cup rolled oats
- 2 cups water
- 1/2 cup mixed fresh fruit (e.g. berries, sliced banana, diced apple)
- 1/4 cup mixed nuts (e.g. almonds, walnuts, pecans)
- 1 tsp honey (optional)

Instructions:

1. In a medium saucepan, bring the water to a boil.

2. Stir in the oats and reduce heat to low. Cook for 5-7 minutes, stirring occasionally, until the oats are soft and creamy.

3. Remove the saucepan from heat and stir in the mixed fruit and nuts.

4. Serve hot, drizzled with honey if desired.

GREEK YOGURT PARFAIT WITH GRANOLA AND BERRIES

Ingredients:

- 1 cup Greek yogurt
- 1/2 cup granola

- 1 cup mixed fresh berries (e.g. strawberries, blueberries, raspberries)
- 1 tsp honey (optional)

Instructions:

1. In a clear glass or bowl, layer the Greek yogurt, granola, and mixed berries.

2. Repeat the layering process until all the ingredients are used up.

3. Drizzle with honey if desired and serve immediately.

VEGETABLE OMELETTE WITH WHOLE WHEAT TOAST

Ingredients:

- 3 eggs
- 1/2 cup mixed chopped vegetables (e.g. bell pepper, onion, mushroom, spinach)
- 1 tsp olive oil
- Salt and pepper, to taste
- 2 slices whole wheat bread
- Butter or margarine, for spreading

Instructions:

1. In a medium bowl, whisk together the eggs and season with salt and pepper.

2. In a non-stick pan, heat the olive oil over medium heat. Add the mixed vegetables and sauté until tender, about 5 minutes.

3. Pour the eggs into the pan with the vegetables and use a spatula to spread the mixture evenly. Cook for 2-3 minutes, or until the bottom is set and the top is slightly runny.

4. Use the spatula to carefully fold the omelette in half and slide onto a plate.

5. Toast the whole wheat bread and spread with butter or margarine. Serve alongside the omelette.

AVOCADO TOAST
WITH A POACHED EGG

Ingredients:

- 2 slices whole grain bread
- 1 ripe avocado, mashed
- Salt and pepper, to taste
- 2 eggs
- Vinegar (for poaching eggs)

Instructions:

1. Toast the whole grain bread to your desired level of crispiness.

2. Spread the mashed avocado onto the toasted bread and season with salt and pepper.

3. Fill a medium saucepan with water and bring to a simmer. Add a splash of vinegar to the water.

4. Crack an egg into a small bowl, then gently slide it into the simmering water. Repeat with the second egg.

5. Cook the eggs for 3-4 minutes, or until the whites are set and the yolks are still runny.

6. Use a slotted spoon to remove the eggs from the water and place one on top of each slice of avocado toast. Serve immediately.

BANANA WALNUT PANCAKES

Ingredients:

- 1 cup all-purpose flour
- 2 tbsp sugar
- 2 tsp baking powder
- 1/2 tsp salt
- 1 cup milk
- 1 egg
- 2 tbsp melted butter
- 1 ripe banana, mashed
- 1/2 cup chopped walnuts

Instructions:

1. In a large bowl, whisk together the flour, sugar, baking powder, and salt.

2. In a separate bowl, whisk together the milk, egg, melted butter, and mashed banana.

3. Add the wet ingredients to the dry ingredients and stir until just combined (the batter will be lumpy).

4. Stir in the chopped walnuts.

5. Heat a non-stick pan or griddle over medium heat. Scoop 1/4 cup of batter onto the pan for each pancake. Cook until bubbles form on the surface and the edges start to look set, about 2-3 minutes.

6. Flip the pancakes and cook for another 1-2 minutes, or until lightly golden brown on both sides.

7. Serve with your desired toppings and syrup.

QUINOA PORRIDGE WITH ALMONDS AND HONEY

Ingredients:

- 1 cup quinoa
- 2 cups water
- 1/2 tsp salt
- 1/4 cup chopped almonds
- 1 tbsp honey (optional)

Instructions:

1. Rinse the quinoa in a fine mesh strainer and drain well.

2. In a medium saucepan, bring the water to a boil and stir in the quinoa and salt.

3. Reduce heat to low, cover the saucepan with a lid, and simmer for 15-20 minutes, or until the quinoa is tender and the water is absorbed.

4. Stir in the chopped almonds and serve hot, drizzled with honey if desired.

SPINACH AND FETA
BREAKFAST WRAP

Ingredients:

- 4 large eggs
- 1 cup fresh spinach leaves
- 1/4 cup crumbled feta cheese
- Salt and pepper, to taste
- 4 large tortillas

Instructions:

1. In a medium bowl, whisk together the eggs and season with salt and pepper.

2. In a non-stick pan, heat a small amount of oil over medium heat. Pour in the eggs and use a spatula to scramble until cooked through, about 3-5 minutes.

3. Stir in the fresh spinach leaves and crumbled feta cheese into the eggs until the spinach is wilted and the feta is melted.

4. Warm the tortillas in a dry pan or in the microwave for 10-15 seconds until soft and pliable.

5. Spoon the egg mixture onto the center of each tortilla, roll up tightly, and serve immediately.

WHOLE-GRAIN CEREAL
WITH MILK AND FRUIT

Ingredients:

- 1 cup whole-grain cereal
- 1 cup milk

- 1/2 cup mixed fresh fruit (e.g. berries, sliced banana, diced apple)

Instructions:

1. Pour the cereal into a bowl.

2. Pour the milk over the cereal and let sit for 1-2 minutes to soften the cereal.

3. Top the cereal with the mixed fruit and serve immediately.

SMOOTHIE WITH MIXED BERRIES, BANANA, AND PROTEIN POWDER

Ingredients:

- 1 cup mixed frozen berries (e.g. strawberries, blueberries, raspberries)
- 1 ripe banana, peeled and frozen
- 1 scoop protein powder
- 1 cup unsweetened almond milk
- 1 tsp honey (optional)

Instructions:

1. Add the mixed frozen berries, frozen banana, protein powder, and almond milk to a blender.

2. Blend on high speed until smooth and creamy, about 1-2 minutes.

3. If the smoothie is too thick, add more almond milk as needed until desired consistency is reached.

4. Sweeten with honey if desired and serve immediately.

SCRAMBLED EGGS WITH
SMOKED SALMON AND CHIVES

Ingredients:

- 4 large eggs
- 1/4 cup milk
- Salt and pepper, to taste
- 2 oz smoked salmon, chopped
- 1 tbsp chopped chives
- Butter or oil, for frying

Instructions:

1. In a medium bowl, whisk together the eggs, milk, salt, and pepper until well combined.

2. In a non-stick pan, heat a small amount of butter or oil over medium heat. Pour in the egg mixture and use a spatula to scramble until cooked through, about 3-5 minutes.

3. Stir in the chopped smoked salmon and chives into the eggs until well combined.

4. Serve immediately and enjoy!

SOUPS

CHICKEN NOODLE SOUP

Ingredients:

- 1 lb boneless, skinless chicken breast, cut into small pieces
- 2 tbsp olive oil
- 1 onion, chopped
- 2 carrots, chopped
- 2 celery stalks, chopped
- 2 cloves garlic, minced
- 8 cups chicken broth
- 1 tsp dried thyme
- 1 tsp dried basil
- 1 tsp salt
- 1/2 tsp black pepper
- 8 oz egg noodles

Instructions:

1. In a large pot, heat the olive oil over medium heat. Add the chicken and cook until browned on all sides, about 5 minutes.

2. Add the onion, carrots, celery, and garlic to the pot. Cook until the vegetables are soft, about 5 minutes.

3. Add the chicken broth, thyme, basil, salt, and pepper to the pot. Bring to a boil, then reduce heat and simmer for 10 minutes.

4. Add the egg noodles to the pot and cook until they are tender, about 10 minutes.

5. Serve hot and enjoy!

LENTIL AND VEGETABLE SOUP

Ingredients:

- 1 cup lentils
- 2 tbsp olive oil
- 1 onion, chopped
- 2 carrots, chopped
- 2 celery stalks, chopped
- 2 cloves garlic, minced
- 8 cups vegetable broth
- 1 tsp dried thyme
- 1 tsp dried basil
- 1 tsp salt
- 1/2 tsp black pepper
- 1 zucchini, chopped
- 1 can diced tomatoes

Instructions:

1. Rinse the lentils and set aside.

2. In a large pot, heat the olive oil over medium heat. Add the onion, carrots, celery, and garlic to the pot. Cook until the vegetables are soft, about 5 minutes.

3. Add the vegetable broth, thyme, basil, salt, and pepper to the pot. Bring to a boil, then reduce heat and simmer for 10 minutes.

4. Add the lentils and zucchini to the pot and cook until the lentils are soft, about 20 minutes.

5. Add the diced tomatoes to the pot and cook for 5 minutes.

6. Serve hot and enjoy!

CREAM OF MUSHROOM SOUP

Ingredients:

- 1 lb mushrooms, sliced
- 2 tbsp butter
- 1 onion, chopped
- 2 cloves garlic, minced
- 2 tbsp all-purpose flour
- 4 cups chicken or vegetable broth
- 1 cup heavy cream
- 1 tsp salt
- 1/2 tsp black pepper

Instructions:

1. In a large pot, melt the butter over medium heat. Add the mushrooms, onion, and garlic to the pot. Cook until the vegetables are soft, about 5 minutes.

2. Add the flour to the pot and stir to combine. Cook for 2 minutes, stirring constantly.

3. Gradually add the broth to the pot, stirring constantly, until the mixture is smooth.

4. Bring the mixture to a boil, then reduce heat and simmer for 10 minutes.

5. Stir in the heavy cream, salt, and pepper. Cook until heated through, about 5 minutes.

6. Serve hot and enjoy!

TOMATO AND BASIL SOUP

Ingredients:

- 2 tbsp olive oil
- 1 onion, chopped
- 2 cloves garlic, minced
- 1 can diced tomatoes
- 4 cups chicken or vegetable broth
- 1 tsp dried basil
- 1 tsp salt
- 1/2 tsp black pepper
- 1/4 cup fresh basil, chopped

Instructions:

1. In a large pot, heat the olive oil over medium heat. Add the onion and garlic to the pot. Cook until the vegetables are soft, about 5 minutes.

2. Add the diced tomatoes, broth, dried basil, salt, and pepper to the pot. Bring to a boil, then reduce heat and simmer for 10 minutes.

3. Stir in the fresh basil and cook for 2 minutes.

4. Serve hot and enjoy!

MINESTRONE SOUP

Ingredients:

- 2 tbsp olive oil
- 1 onion, chopped
- 2 carrots, chopped

- 2 celery stalks, chopped
- 2 cloves garlic, minced

  1 can diced tomatoes

- 8 cups vegetable broth
- 1 tsp dried thyme
- 1 tsp dried basil
- 1 tsp salt
- 1/2 tsp black pepper
- 1 cup small pasta shapes
- 1 cup cooked and drained kidney beans
- 1 cup chopped kale or spinach

Instructions:

1. In a large pot, heat the olive oil over medium heat. Add the onion, carrots, celery, and garlic to the pot. Cook until the vegetables are soft, about 5 minutes.

2. Add the diced tomatoes, broth, thyme, basil, salt, and pepper to the pot. Bring to a boil, then reduce heat and simmer for 10 minutes.

3. Add the pasta to the pot and cook until it is tender, about 10 minutes.

4. Stir in the kidney beans and kale or spinach. Cook until heated through, about 5 minutes.

5. Serve hot and enjoy!

BUTTERNUT SQUASH
AND APPLE SOUP

Ingredients:

- 1 butternut squash, peeled and chopped
- 2 apples, peeled and chopped
- 2 tbsp butter
- 1 onion, chopped
- 2 cloves garlic, minced
- 4 cups chicken or vegetable broth
- 1 tsp dried thyme
- 1 tsp salt
- 1/2 tsp black pepper
- 1 cup heavy cream

Instructions:

1. In a large pot, melt the butter over medium heat. Add the onion and garlic to the pot. Cook until the vegetables are soft, about 5 minutes.

2. Add the butternut squash, apples, broth, thyme, salt, and pepper to the pot. Bring to a boil, then reduce heat and simmer for 20 minutes.

3. Use an immersion blender to puree the mixture until it is smooth.

4. Stir in the heavy cream and cook until heated through, about 5 minutes.

5. Serve hot and enjoy!

SPLIT PEA AND HAM SOUP

Ingredients:

- 1 lb dried split peas
- 1 lb ham, cubed
- 2 tbsp olive oil
- 1 onion, chopped
- 2 carrots, chopped
- 2 celery stalks, chopped
- 2 cloves garlic, minced
- 8 cups chicken or vegetable broth
- 1 tsp dried thyme
- 1 tsp dried basil
- 1 tsp salt
- 1/2 tsp black pepper

Instructions:

1. Rinse the split peas and set aside.

2. In a large pot, heat the olive oil over medium heat. Add the onion, carrots, celery, and garlic to the pot. Cook until the vegetables are soft, about 5 minutes.

3. Add the split peas, ham, broth, thyme, basil, salt, and pepper to the pot. Bring to a boil, then reduce heat and simmer for 30 minutes or until the split peas are soft.

4. Use an immersion blender to puree the mixture until it is smooth.

5. Serve hot and enjoy!

CARROT GINGER SOUP

Ingredients:

- 1 lb carrots, chopped
- 2 tbsp ginger, grated
- 2 tbsp butter
- 1 onion, chopped
- 2 cloves garlic, minced
- 4 cups chicken or vegetable broth
- 1 tsp salt
- 1/2 tsp black pepper
- 1 cup heavy cream

Instructions:

1. In a large pot, melt the butter over medium heat. Add the onion and garlic to the pot. Cook until the vegetables are soft, about 5 minutes.

2. Add the carrots, ginger, broth, salt, and pepper to the pot. Bring to a boil, then reduce heat and simmer for 20 minutes or until the carrots are soft.

3. Use an immersion blender to puree the mixture until it is smooth.

4. Stir in the heavy cream and cook until heated through, about 5 minutes.

5. Serve hot and enjoy!

POTATO LEEK SOUP

Ingredients:

- 2 lbs potatoes, peeled and chopped

- 2 leeks, sliced
- 2 tbsp butter
- 4 cups chicken or vegetable broth
- 1 tsp salt
- 1/2 tsp black pepper
- 1 cup heavy cream

Instructions:

1. In a large pot, melt the butter over medium heat. Add the leeks to the pot. Cook until they are soft, about 5 minutes.

2. Add the potatoes, broth, salt, and pepper to the pot. Bring to a boil, then reduce heat and simmer for 20 minutes or until the potatoes are soft.

3. Use an immersion blender to puree the mixture until it is smooth.

4. Stir in the heavy cream and cook until heated through, about 5 minutes.

5. Serve hot and enjoy!

WHITE BEAN AND KALE SOUP

Ingredients:

- 1 lb white beans, soaked overnight
- 2 tbsp olive oil
- 1 onion, chopped
- 2 carrots, chopped
- 2 celery stalks, chopped
- 2 cloves garlic, minced
- 8 cups chicken or vegetable broth
- 1 tsp dried thyme

- 1 tsp dried basil
- 1 tsp salt
- 1/2 tsp black pepper
- 1 cup chopped kale

Instructions:

1. In a large pot, heat the olive oil over medium heat. Add the onion, carrots, celery, and garlic to the pot. Cook until the vegetables are soft, about 5 minutes.

2. Add the white beans, broth, thyme, basil, salt, and pepper to the pot. Bring to a boil, then reduce heat and simmer for 30 minutes or until the beans are soft.

3. Stir in the kale and cook until wilted, about 5 minutes.

4. Serve hot and enjoy!

STEWS

BEEF AND VEGETABLE STEW

Ingredients:

- 2 lbs beef stew meat, cut into 1-inch pieces
- 1 large onion, chopped
- 3 cloves of garlic, minced
- 2 large carrots, sliced
- 2 large potatoes, peeled and diced
- 1 cup frozen peas
- 1 cup frozen corn
- 1 cup beef broth
- 1 cup tomato sauce
- 1 tsp dried thyme
- 1 tsp dried rosemary
- 1 tsp salt
- 1/2 tsp black pepper

Instructions:

1. In a large pot or Dutch oven, heat 2 tbsp of oil over medium heat. Add the beef and cook until browned on all sides, about 5-7 minutes. Remove the beef from the pot and set aside.

2. Add the onion, garlic, carrots, and potatoes to the same pot and cook until the onion is soft and translucent, about 5 minutes.

3. Return the beef to the pot and add the peas, corn, beef broth, tomato sauce, thyme, rosemary, salt, and pepper. Stir to combine.

4. Bring the stew to a boil, then reduce heat to low and cover the pot. Simmer for 1-1 1/2 hours, or until the beef is tender and the vegetables are cooked through.

5. Serve hot and enjoy!

CHICKEN AND RICE STEW

Ingredients:

- 2 lbs boneless chicken breast, cut into 1-inch pieces
- 1 large onion, chopped
- 3 cloves of garlic, minced
- 2 cups chicken broth
- 1 cup long-grain white rice
- 1 cup diced carrots
- 1 cup frozen green beans
- 1 cup diced tomatoes
- 1 tsp dried thyme
- 1 tsp dried basil
- 1 tsp salt
- 1/2 tsp black pepper

Instructions:

1. In a large pot or Dutch oven, heat 2 tbsp of oil over medium heat. Add the chicken and cook until browned on all sides, about 5-7 minutes. Remove the chicken from the pot and set aside.

2. Add the onion, garlic, carrots, and green beans to the same pot and cook until the onion is soft and translucent, about 5 minutes.

3. Return the chicken to the pot and add the chicken broth, rice, diced tomatoes, thyme, basil, salt, and pepper. Stir to combine.

4. Bring the stew to a boil, then reduce heat to low and cover the pot. Simmer for 20-25 minutes, or until the rice is cooked and the chicken is tender.

5. Serve hot and enjoy!

RATATOUILLE

Ingredients:

- 2 large eggplants, diced
- 2 large zucchinis, diced
- 2 large bell peppers, diced
- 1 large onion, chopped
- 4 cloves of garlic, minced
- 1 cup diced tomatoes
- 2 tbsp tomato paste
- 1 tsp dried thyme
- 1 tsp dried basil
- 1 tsp salt
- 1/2 tsp black pepper

Instructions:

1. In a large pot or Dutch oven, heat 2 tbsp of oil over medium heat. Add the eggplants, zucchinis, bell peppers, and onion and cook until soft and slightly browned, about 10 minutes.

2. Add the garlic, diced tomatoes, tomato paste, thyme, basil, salt, and pepper. Stir to combine.

3. Reduce heat to low and cover the pot. Simmer for 30-35 minutes, or until the vegetables are tender and the sauce has thickened.

4. Serve hot and enjoy!

MOROCCAN CHICKPEA STEW

Ingredients:

- 2 cans of chickpeas, drained and rinsed
- 1 large onion, chopped
- 3 cloves of garlic, minced
- 1 cup diced carrots
- 1 cup diced sweet potatoes
- 1 cup diced tomatoes
- 1 tsp ground cumin
- 1 tsp ground cinnamon
- 1 tsp paprika
- 1 tsp salt
- 1/2 tsp black pepper

Instructions:

1. In a large pot or Dutch oven, heat 2 tbsp of oil over medium heat. Add the onion, garlic, carrots, and sweet potatoes and cook until the onion is soft and translucent, about 5 minutes.

2. Add the chickpeas, diced tomatoes, cumin, cinnamon, paprika, salt, and pepper. Stir to combine.

3. Reduce heat to low and cover the pot. Simmer for 20-25 minutes, or until the vegetables are tender and the stew is heated through.

4. Serve hot and enjoy!

IRISH LAMB STEW

Ingredients:

- 2 lbs lamb stew meat, cut into 1-inch pieces
- 1 large onion, chopped
- 3 cloves of garlic, minced
- 2 large potatoes, peeled and diced
- 2 cups beef broth
- 1 cup frozen peas
- 1 tsp dried thyme
- 1 tsp dried rosemary
- 1 tsp salt
- 1/2 tsp black pepper

Instructions:

1. In a large pot or Dutch oven, heat 2 tbsp of oil over medium heat. Add the lamb and cook until browned on all sides, about 5-7 minutes. Remove the lamb from the pot and set aside.

2. Add the onion, garlic, and potatoes to the same pot and cook until the onion is soft and translucent, about 5 minutes.

3. Return the lamb to the pot and add the beef broth, peas, thyme, rosemary, salt, and pepper. Stir to combine.

4. Bring the stew to a boil, then reduce heat to low and cover the pot. Simmer for 1-1 1/2 hours, or until the lamb is tender and the vegetables are cooked through.

5. Serve hot and enjoy!

SEAFOOD GUMBO

Ingredients:

- 1 lb shrimp, peeled and deveined
- 1 lb crab meat
- 1 large onion, chopped
- 3 cloves of garlic, minced
- 2 large bell peppers, diced
- 2 cups chicken broth
- 1 cup diced tomatoes
- 1 tsp Cajun seasoning
- 1 tsp dried thyme
- 1 tsp salt
- 1/2 tsp black pepper

Instructions:

1. In a large pot or Dutch oven, heat 2 tbsp of oil over medium heat. Add the onion, garlic, and bell peppers and cook until the onion is soft and translucent, about 5 minutes.

2. Add the chicken broth, diced tomatoes, Cajun seasoning, thyme, salt, and pepper. Stir to combine.

3. Bring the gumbo to a boil, then reduce heat to low and cover the pot. Simmer for 20-25 minutes, or until the vegetables are tender.

4. Add the shrimp and crab meat and cook until the shrimp are pink and the crab is heated through, about 5-7 minutes.

5. Serve hot and enjoy!

HUNGARIAN GOULASH

Ingredients:

- 2 lbs beef stew meat, cut into 1-inch pieces
- 1 large onion, chopped
- 3 cloves of garlic, minced
- 2 large carrots, sliced
- 2 large potatoes, peeled and diced
- 1 cup diced tomatoes
- 1 cup beef broth
- 1 tbsp paprika
- 1 tsp dried thyme
- 1 tsp salt
- 1/2 tsp black pepper

Instructions:

1. In a large pot or Dutch oven, heat 2 tbsp of oil over medium heat. Add the beef and cook until browned on all sides, about 5-7 minutes. Remove the beef from the pot and set aside.

2. Add the onion, garlic, carrots, and potatoes to the same pot and cook until the onion is soft and translucent, about 5 minutes.

3. Return the beef to the pot and add the diced tomatoes, beef broth, paprika, thyme, salt, and pepper. Stir to combine.

4. Bring the goulash to a boil, then reduce heat to low and cover the pot. Simmer for 1-1 1/2 hours, or until the beef is tender and the vegetables are cooked through.

5. Serve hot and enjoy!

PORK AND GREEN CHILE STEW

Ingredients:

- 2 lbs pork stew meat, cut into 1-inch pieces
- 1 large onion, chopped
- 3 cloves of garlic, minced
- 2 large carrots, sliced
- 2 large potatoes, peeled and diced
- 2 cans of green chiles
- 1 cup chicken broth
- 1 tsp dried thyme
- 1 tsp dried cumin
- 1 tsp salt
- 1/2 tsp black pepper

Instructions:

1. In a large pot or Dutch oven, heat 2 tbsp of oil over medium heat. Add the pork and cook until browned on all sides, about 5-7 minutes. Remove the pork from the pot and set aside.

2. Add the onion, garlic, carrots, and potatoes to the same pot and cook until the onion is soft and translucent, about 5 minutes.

3. Return the pork to the pot and add the green chiles, chicken broth, thyme, cumin, salt, and pepper. Stir to combine.

4. Bring the stew to a boil, then reduce heat to low and cover the pot. Simmer for 1-1 1/2 hours, or until the pork is tender and the vegetables are cooked through.

5. Serve hot and enjoy!

MEDITERRANEAN FISH STEW

Ingredients:

- 1 lb fish fillets, cut into 1-inch pieces
- 1 large onion, chopped
- 3 cloves of garlic, minced
- 1 cup diced tomatoes
- 1 cup chicken broth
- 1 cup white wine
- 1 tsp dried thyme
- 1 tsp dried oregano
- 1 tsp salt
- 1/2 tsp black pepper

Instructions:

1. In a large pot or Dutch oven, heat 2 tbsp of oil over medium heat. Add the onion and garlic and cook until the onion is soft and translucent, about 5 minutes.

2. Add the diced tomatoes, chicken broth, white wine, thyme, oregano, salt, and pepper. Stir to combine.

3. Bring the stew to a boil, then reduce heat to low and cover the pot. Simmer for 10-15 minutes, or until the sauce has thickened slightly.

4. Add the fish and cook until the fish is opaque and cooked through, about 5-7 minutes.

5. Serve hot and enjoy!

ROOT VEGETABLE AND BARLEY STEW

Ingredients:

- 2 large carrots, sliced
- 2 large parsnips, sliced
- 2 large turnips, peeled and diced
- 1 large onion, chopped
- 3 cloves of garlic, minced
- 1 cup barley
- 4 cups chicken broth
- 1 tsp dried thyme
- 1 tsp dried rosemary
- 1 tsp salt
- 1/2 tsp black pepper

Instructions:

1. In a large pot or Dutch oven, heat 2 tbsp of oil over medium heat. Add the onion and garlic and cook until the onion is soft and translucent, about 5 minutes.

2. Add the carrots, parsnips, turnips, barley, chicken broth, thyme, rosemary, salt, and pepper. Stir to combine.

3. Bring the stew to a boil, then reduce heat to low and cover the pot. Simmer for 40-45 minutes, or until the vegetables are tender and the barley is cooked through.

4. Serve hot and enjoy!

MAIN DISHES

BAKED SALMON WITH LEMON AND DILL

Ingredients:

- 2 salmon fillets
- 2 tablespoons olive oil
- 2 lemons, sliced
- 1/4 cup chopped fresh dill
- Salt and pepper, to taste

Instructions:

1. Preheat oven to 400°F. Line a baking sheet with parchment paper or aluminum foil.

2. Place the salmon fillets on the prepared baking sheet and brush with olive oil. Season with salt and pepper to taste.

3. Top each fillet with lemon slices and sprinkle with dill.

4. Bake for 12-15 minutes, or until the salmon is fully cooked and flaky.

5. Serve with additional lemon wedges and freshly chopped dill, if desired.

CHICKEN PICCATA

Ingredients:

- 2 boneless, skinless chicken breasts

- 1/2 cup all-purpose flour
- Salt and pepper, to taste
- 2 tablespoons olive oil
- 2 garlic cloves, minced
- 1 cup chicken broth
- 1/2 cup lemon juice
- 2 tablespoons capers
- 2 tablespoons unsalted butter
- Chopped fresh parsley, for garnish

Instructions:

1. Season the chicken breasts with salt and pepper and coat in flour, shaking off any excess.

2. In a large skillet, heat the olive oil over medium-high heat. Add the chicken breasts and cook until browned on both sides, about 5-7 minutes per side.

3. Remove the chicken from the skillet and set aside. Add the garlic to the same skillet and cook until fragrant, about 30 seconds.

4. Add the chicken broth, lemon juice, and capers to the skillet, scraping the bottom of the pan to release any browned bits.

5. Return the chicken to the skillet and spoon some of the sauce over the top. Simmer for 5-7 minutes, or until the chicken is fully cooked and the sauce has thickened slightly.

6. Remove from heat and stir in the butter until melted. Serve with additional sauce and a sprinkle of fresh parsley, if desired.

VEGETARIAN LASAGNA

Ingredients:

- 9 lasagna noodles
- 1 tablespoon olive oil
- 1 onion, diced
- 2 garlic cloves, minced
- 2 cups chopped vegetables (such as zucchini, bell peppers, and mushrooms)
- 1 (24 oz) jar marinara sauce
- 1 (15 oz) container ricotta cheese
- 1 cup shredded mozzarella cheese
- 1/4 cup grated parmesan cheese
- 1 egg
- Salt and pepper, to taste

Instructions:

1. Preheat oven to 375°F. Cook the lasagna noodles according to package instructions and set aside.

2. In a large skillet, heat the olive oil over medium heat. Add the onion and cook until soft and translucent, about 5-7 minutes.

3. Add the garlic and chopped vegetables to the skillet and cook until tender, about 5-7 minutes.

4. In a large bowl, mix together the ricotta cheese, 1/2 cup mozzarella cheese, parmesan cheese, egg, salt, and pepper.

5. In a 9x13 inch baking dish, spread a layer of marinara sauce on the bottom. Place 3 cooked lasagna noodles on top, followed by a layer of the vegetable mixture and a layer of the ricotta mixture.

6. Repeat the layers until all ingredients are used, ending with a layer of marinara sauce and a sprinkle of mozzarella cheese on top.

7. Cover the dish with aluminum foil and bake for 25 minutes. Remove the foil and bake for an additional 10-15 minutes, or until the cheese is melted and bubbly.

PORK TENDERLOIN WITH APPLES AND ONIONS

Ingredients:

- 1 pork tenderloin (about 1 lb)
- Salt and pepper, to taste
- 2 tablespoons olive oil
- 1 large onion, sliced
- 2 apples, peeled, cored, and sliced
- 1/4 cup apple cider
- 1/4 cup chicken broth
- 1 tablespoon Dijon mustard
- 1 tablespoon honey
- 2 tablespoons chopped fresh thyme

Instructions:

1. Preheat oven to 400°F. Season the pork tenderloin with salt and pepper.

2. In a large oven-safe skillet, heat the olive oil over medium-high heat. Add the pork.

3. Cook until browned on all sides, about 5-7 minutes.

4. Remove the pork from the skillet and set aside. Add the onion and apple to the same skillet and cook until softened, about 5-7 minutes.

5. In a small bowl, whisk together the apple cider, chicken broth, Dijon mustard, honey, and thyme. Pour the mixture over the apples and onions in the skillet.

6. Place the pork back in the skillet and spoon some of the sauce over the top. Bake for 25-30 minutes, or until the pork is fully cooked and the internal temperature reaches 145°F.

7. Serve the pork with additional sauce and a sprinkle of fresh thyme, if desired.

SHRIMP AND VEGETABLE STIR-FRY

Ingredients:

- 1 lb raw shrimp, peeled and deveined
- 2 tablespoons vegetable oil
- 1 onion, sliced
- 2 garlic cloves, minced
- 2 cups chopped vegetables (such as bell peppers, carrots, and broccoli)
- 2 tablespoons soy sauce
- 1 tablespoon cornstarch
- 1 tablespoon honey
- 1 teaspoon sesame oil
- 1/4 teaspoon red pepper flakes (optional)
- Chopped green onions, for garnish

Instructions:

1. In a small bowl, whisk together the soy sauce, cornstarch, honey, sesame oil, and red pepper flakes (if using).

2. In a large wok or skillet, heat the vegetable oil over high heat. Add the onion and garlic and cook until fragrant, about 30 seconds.

3. Add the chopped vegetables and cook until tender, about 5-7 minutes.

4. Add the shrimp to the wok and cook until pink and fully cooked, about 2-3 minutes.

5. Pour the sauce over the shrimp and vegetables and stir to combine. Cook until the sauce has thickened, about 2-3 minutes.

6. Serve with rice or noodles and garnish with chopped green onions, if desired.

EGGPLANT PARMESAN

Ingredients:

- 2 medium eggplants, sliced into rounds
- Salt and pepper, to taste
- 1 cup all-purpose flour
- 2 eggs, beaten
- 2 cups Italian-seasoned breadcrumbs
- 1/4 cup olive oil
- 1 (24 oz) jar marinara sauce
- 1 cup shredded mozzarella cheese
- 1/4 cup grated parmesan cheese
- Fresh basil leaves, for garnish

Instructions:

1. Preheat oven to 375°F. Line a baking sheet with parchment paper or aluminum foil.

2. Place the eggplant slices in a single layer on the prepared baking sheet and sprinkle with salt and pepper. Bake for 15-20 minutes, or until tender and lightly browned.

3. In three separate bowls, place the flour, beaten eggs, and breadcrumbs. Dip each eggplant slice first in the flour, then in the eggs, and finally in the breadcrumbs, making sure to fully coat each slice.

4. In a large skillet, heat the olive oil over medium-high heat. Add the breaded eggplant slices and cook until golden brown on both sides, about 3-4 minutes per side.

5. In a 9x13 inch baking dish, spread a layer of marinara sauce on the bottom. Place a layer of the cooked eggplant slices on top, followed by another layer of marinara sauce and a sprinkle of mozzarella and parmesan cheese.

6. Repeat the layers until all ingredients are used, ending with a layer of marinara sauce and a sprinkle of mozzarella and parmesan cheese on top.

7. Cover the dish with aluminum foil and bake for 25 minutes. Remove the foil and bake for an additional 10-15 minutes, or until the cheese is melted and bubbly.

8. Serve with fresh basil leaves, if desired.

STUFFED BELL PEPPERS

Ingredients:

- 4 large bell peppers, sliced in half and seeded
- 1 tablespoon olive oil
- 1 onion, diced
- 2 garlic cloves, minced

- 1 lb ground beef or turkey
- 1 (14 oz) can diced tomatoes
- 1 cup cooked brown rice
- 1/4 cup chopped fresh parsley
- 1 cup shredded cheddar cheese
- Salt and pepper, to taste

Instructions:

1. Preheat oven to 375°F. Line a baking sheet with parchment paper or aluminum foil.

2. In a large skillet, heat the olive oil over medium heat. Add the onion and cook until soft and translucent, about 5-7 minutes.

3. Add the garlic, ground beef or turkey, and diced tomatoes to the skillet. Cook until the meat is fully cooked and browned, about 10-12 minutes.

4. Stir in the cooked rice, parsley, salt, and pepper. Remove from heat and set aside.

5. Place the pepper halves on the prepared baking sheet and fill each half with the meat and rice mixture.

6. Top each stuffed pepper with shredded cheddar cheese. Bake for 25-30 minutes, or until the peppers are tender and the cheese is melted and bubbly.

7. Serve hot and enjoy!

BAKED SALMON WITH LEMON AND DILL

Ingredients:

- 2 salmon fillets
- 2 tablespoons olive oil
- 2 lemons, sliced
- 1/4 cup chopped fresh dill
- Salt and pepper, to taste

Instructions:

1. Preheat oven to 400°F. Line a baking sheet with parchment paper or aluminum foil.

2. Place the salmon fillets on the prepared baking sheet and brush with olive oil. Season with salt and pepper to taste.

3. Top each fillet with lemon slices and sprinkle with dill.

4. Bake for 12-15 minutes, or until the salmon is fully cooked and flaky.

5. Serve with additional lemon wedges and freshly chopped dill, if desired.

CHICKEN PICCATA

Ingredients:

- 2 boneless, skinless chicken breasts
- 1/2 cup all-purpose flour
- Salt and pepper, to taste
- 2 tablespoons olive oil
- 2 garlic cloves, minced

- 1 cup chicken broth
- 1/2 cup lemon juice
- 2 tablespoons capers
- 2 tablespoons unsalted butter
- Chopped fresh parsley, for garnish

Instructions:

1. Season the chicken breasts with salt and pepper and coat in flour, shaking off any excess.

2. In a large skillet, heat the olive oil over medium-high heat. Add the chicken breasts and cook until browned on both sides, about 5-7 minutes per side.

3. Remove the chicken from the skillet and set aside. Add the garlic to the same skillet and cook until fragrant, about 30 seconds.

4. Add the chicken broth, lemon juice, and capers to the skillet, scraping the bottom of the pan to release any browned bits.

5. Return the chicken to the skillet and spoon some of the sauce over the top. Simmer for 5-7 minutes, or until the chicken is fully cooked and the sauce has thickened slightly.

6. Remove from heat and stir in the butter until melted. Serve with additional sauce and a sprinkle of fresh parsley, if desired.

VEGETARIAN LASAGNA

Ingredients:

- 9 lasagna noodles

- 1 tablespoon olive oil
- 1 onion, diced
- 2 garlic cloves, minced
- 2 cups chopped vegetables (such as zucchini, bell peppers, and mushrooms)
- 1 (24 oz) jar marinara sauce
- 1 (15 oz) container ricotta cheese
- 1 cup shredded mozzarella cheese
- 1/4 cup grated parmesan cheese
- 1 egg
- Salt and pepper, to taste

Instructions:

1. Preheat oven to 375°F. Cook the lasagna noodles according to package instructions and set aside.

2. In a large skillet, heat the olive oil over medium heat. Add the onion and cook until soft and translucent, about 5-7 minutes.

3. Add the garlic and chopped vegetables to the skillet and cook until tender, about 5-7 minutes.

4. In a large bowl, mix together the ricotta cheese, 1/2 cup mozzarella cheese, parmesan cheese, egg, salt, and pepper.

5. In a 9x13 inch baking dish, spread a layer of marinara sauce on the bottom. Place 3 cooked lasagna noodles on top, followed by a layer of the vegetable mixture and a layer of the ricotta mixture.

6. Repeat the layers until all ingredients are used, ending with a layer of marinara sauce and a sprinkle of mozzarella cheese on top.

7. Cover the dish with aluminum foil and bake for 25 minutes. Remove the foil and bake for an additional 10-15 minutes, or until the cheese is melted and bubbly.

PORK TENDERLOIN WITH APPLES AND ONIONS

Ingredients:

- 1 pork tenderloin (about 1 lb)
- Salt and pepper, to taste
- 2 tablespoons olive oil
- 1 large onion, sliced
- 2 apples, peeled, cored, and sliced
- 1/4 cup apple cider
- 1/4 cup chicken broth
- 1 tablespoon Dijon mustard
- 1 tablespoon honey
- 2 tablespoons chopped fresh thyme

Instructions:

1. Preheat oven to 400°F. Season the pork tenderloin with salt and pepper.

2. In a large oven-safe skillet, heat the olive oil over medium-high heat. Add the pork.

3. Cook until browned on all sides, about 5-7 minutes.

4. Remove the pork from the skillet and set aside. Add the onion and apple to the same skillet and cook until softened, about 5-7 minutes.

5. In a small bowl, whisk together the apple cider, chicken broth, Dijon mustard, honey, and thyme. Pour the mixture over the apples and onions in the skillet.

6. Place the pork back in the skillet and spoon some of the sauce over the top. Bake for 25-30 minutes, or until the pork is fully cooked and the internal temperature reaches 145°F.

7. Serve the pork with additional sauce and a sprinkle of fresh thyme, if desired.

SHRIMP AND VEGETABLE STIR-FRY

Ingredients:

- 1 lb raw shrimp, peeled and deveined
- 2 tablespoons vegetable oil
- 1 onion, sliced
- 2 garlic cloves, minced
- 2 cups chopped vegetables (such as bell peppers, carrots, and broccoli)
- 2 tablespoons soy sauce
- 1 tablespoon cornstarch
- 1 tablespoon honey
- 1 teaspoon sesame oil
- 1/4 teaspoon red pepper flakes (optional)
- Chopped green onions, for garnish

Instructions:

1. In a small bowl, whisk together the soy sauce, cornstarch, honey, sesame oil, and red pepper flakes (if using).

2. In a large wok or skillet, heat the vegetable oil over high heat. Add the onion and garlic and cook until fragrant, about 30 seconds.

3. Add the chopped vegetables and cook until tender, about 5-7 minutes.

4. Add the shrimp to the wok and cook until pink and fully cooked, about 2-3 minutes.

5. Pour the sauce over the shrimp and vegetables and stir to combine. Cook until the sauce has thickened, about 2-3 minutes.

6. Serve with rice or noodles and garnish with chopped green onions, if desired.

EGGPLANT PARMESAN

Ingredients:

- 2 medium eggplants, sliced into rounds
- Salt and pepper, to taste
- 1 cup all-purpose flour
- 2 eggs, beaten
- 2 cups Italian-seasoned breadcrumbs
- 1/4 cup olive oil
- 1 (24 oz) jar marinara sauce
- 1 cup shredded mozzarella cheese
- 1/4 cup grated parmesan cheese
- Fresh basil leaves, for garnish

Instructions:

1. Preheat oven to 375°F. Line a baking sheet with parchment paper or aluminum foil.

2. Place the eggplant slices in a single layer on the prepared baking sheet and sprinkle with salt and pepper. Bake for 15-20 minutes, or until tender and lightly browned.

3. In three separate bowls, place the flour, beaten eggs, and breadcrumbs. Dip each eggplant slice first in the flour, then in the eggs, and finally in the breadcrumbs, making sure to fully coat each slice.

4. In a large skillet, heat the olive oil over medium-high heat. Add the breaded eggplant slices and cook until golden brown on both sides, about 3-4 minutes per side.

5. In a 9x13 inch baking dish, spread a layer of marinara sauce on the bottom. Place a layer of the cooked eggplant slices on top, followed by another layer of marinara sauce and a sprinkle of mozzarella and parmesan cheese.

6. Repeat the layers until all ingredients are used, ending with a layer of marinara sauce and a sprinkle of mozzarella and parmesan cheese on top.

7. Cover the dish with aluminum foil and bake for 25 minutes. Remove the foil and bake for an additional 10-15 minutes, or until the cheese is melted and bubbly.

8. Serve with fresh basil leaves, if desired.

STUFFED BELL PEPPERS

Ingredients:

- 4 large bell peppers, sliced in half and seeded
- 1 tablespoon olive oil
- 1 onion, diced
- 2 garlic cloves, minced
- 1 lb ground beef or turkey
- 1 (14 oz) can diced tomatoes
- 1 cup cooked brown rice
- 1/4 cup chopped fresh parsley
- 1 cup shredded cheddar cheese

- Salt and pepper, to taste

Instructions:

1. Preheat oven to 375°F. Line a baking sheet with parchment paper or aluminum foil.

2. In a large skillet, heat the olive oil over medium heat. Add the onion and cook until soft and translucent, about 5-7 minutes.

3. Add the garlic, ground beef or turkey, and diced tomatoes to the skillet. Cook until the meat is fully cooked and browned, about 10-12 minutes.

4. Stir in the cooked rice, parsley, salt, and pepper. Remove from heat and set aside.

5. Place the pepper halves on the prepared baking sheet and fill each half with the meat and rice mixture.

6. Top each stuffed pepper with shredded cheddar cheese. Bake for 25-30 minutes, or until the peppers are tender and the cheese is melted and bubbly.

7. Serve hot and enjoy!

CHICKEN CACCIATORE

Ingredients:

- 4 boneless, skinless chicken breasts
- Salt and pepper, to taste
- 2 tablespoons olive oil
- 1 onion, diced
- 2 garlic cloves, minced
- 1 cup sliced mushrooms

- 1 (14 oz) can diced tomatoes
- 1/2 cup chicken broth
- 1 teaspoon dried basil
- 1 teaspoon dried oregano
- 1/4 teaspoon red pepper flakes (optional)

Instructions:

1. Season the chicken breasts with salt and pepper.

2. In a large skillet, heat the olive oil over medium heat. Add the chicken breasts and cook until browned on both sides and fully cooked, about 6-8 minutes per side.

3. Remove the chicken from the skillet and set aside. Add the onion and garlic to the same skillet and cook until soft and translucent, about 5-7 minutes.

4. Add the mushrooms, diced tomatoes, chicken broth, basil, oregano, and red pepper flakes (if using) to the skillet. Stir to combine.

5. Place the chicken breasts back in the skillet, spooning some of the sauce over the top. Reduce heat to low and let simmer for 10-15 minutes, or until the sauce has thickened slightly and the chicken is fully coated.

6. Serve hot with pasta or rice and additional sauce, if desired.

SPAGHETTI WITH MARINARA SAUCE AND MEATBALLS

Ingredients:

- 1 lb spaghetti
- 1 tablespoon olive oil

- 1 onion, diced
- 2 garlic cloves, minced
- 1 (24 oz) jar marinara sauce
- 1 lb ground beef or turkey
- 1 egg
- 1/4 cup breadcrumbs
- 2 tablespoons grated parmesan cheese
- 1 teaspoon dried basil
- 1 teaspoon dried oregano
- Salt and pepper, to taste

Instructions:

1. Cook the spaghetti according to package instructions and set aside.

2. In a large skillet, heat the olive oil over medium heat. Add the onion and cook until soft and translucent, about 5-7 minutes.

3. Add the garlic and marinara sauce to the skillet and let simmer for 10 minutes.

4. In a separate bowl, mix together the ground beef or turkey, egg, breadcrumbs, parmesan cheese, basil, oregano, salt, and pepper. Form into 1-inch meatballs.

5. Add the meatballs to the skillet with the marinara sauce and let simmer for 15-20 minutes, or until the meatballs are fully cooked and the sauce has thickened slightly.

6. Serve the meatballs and sauce over cooked spaghetti.

SHEPHERD'S PIE

Ingredients:

- 2 lbs potatoes, peeled and chopped
- 1/4 cup milk
- 2 tablespoons butter
- Salt and pepper, to taste
- 1 tablespoon olive oil
- 1 onion, diced
- 2 garlic cloves, minced
- 1 lb ground beef or lamb
- 1 cup frozen mixed vegetables (such as carrots, peas, and corn)
- 1 teaspoon dried thyme
- 1 teaspoon dried rosemary
- 1/2 cup beef broth
- 2 tablespoons flour

Instructions:

1. Preheat oven to 375°F. Line a 9x13 inch baking dish with parchment paper or aluminum foil.

2. In a large pot, boil the potatoes in salted water until tender, about 15-20 minutes. Drain and mash with milk, butter, salt, and pepper.

3. In a large skillet, heat the olive oil over medium heat. Add the onion and cook until soft and translucent, about 5-7 minutes.

4. Add the garlic and ground beef or lamb to the skillet and cook until browned, about 10-12 minutes.

5. Stir in the mixed vegetables, thyme, rosemary, beef broth, and flour. Let simmer for 5-7 minutes, or until the mixture has thickened slightly.

6. Spread the ground beef mixture evenly in the prepared baking dish. Spoon the mashed potatoes over the top, spreading it evenly to cover the beef mixture.

7. Bake for 25-30 minutes, or until the potatoes are lightly browned and the mixture is hot and bubbly.

8. Serve hot and enjoy!

CHICKEN AND VEGETABLE CURRY

Ingredients:

- 1 lb boneless, skinless chicken breasts, diced
- 2 tablespoons olive oil
- 1 onion, diced
- 2 garlic cloves, minced
- 1 teaspoon ginger, grated
- 1 teaspoon turmeric
- 1 teaspoon cumin
- 1 teaspoon coriander
- 1 teaspoon garam masala
- 1 (14 oz) can coconut milk
- 1 cup chicken broth
- 2 cups mixed vegetables (such as carrots, potatoes, and bell peppers)
- Salt and pepper, to taste
- Fresh cilantro, for garnish

Instructions:

1. In a large skillet, heat the olive oil over medium heat. Add the onion and cook until soft and translucent, about 5-7 minutes.

2. Add the garlic, ginger, turmeric, cumin, coriander, and garam masala to the skillet and cook for 1-2 minutes, or until fragrant.

3. Stir in the coconut milk, chicken broth, and mixed vegetables. Let simmer for 10-15 minutes, or until the vegetables are tender and the sauce has thickened slightly.

4. Stir in the diced chicken and let simmer for an additional 10-15 minutes, or until the chicken is fully cooked and the sauce has thickened slightly.

5. Season with salt and pepper to taste.

6. Serve over rice and garnish with fresh cilantro, if desired.

GRILLED CHICKEN WITH MANGO SALSA

Ingredients:

- 4 boneless, skinless chicken breasts
- Salt and pepper, to taste
- 1 mango, peeled and diced
- 1/2 red onion, diced
- 1 jalapeno pepper, seeded and diced
- 2 tablespoons chopped fresh cilantro
- 1 lime, juiced
- 1 tablespoon olive oil

Instructions:

1. Preheat grill to medium-high heat.

2. Season the chicken breasts with salt and pepper.

3. In a small bowl, mix together the diced mango, red onion, jalapeno pepper, cilantro, lime juice, and olive oil to make the salsa.

4. Place the chicken breasts on the grill and cook for 6-8 minutes per side, or until fully cooked and the internal temperature reaches 165°F.

5. Serve the grilled chicken with the mango salsa spooned over the top.

QUINOA-STUFFED TOMATOES

Ingredients:

- 6 large tomatoes
- 1 cup quinoa
- 2 cups chicken or vegetable broth
- 1 tablespoon olive oil
- 1 onion, diced
- 2 garlic cloves, minced
- 1 cup mixed vegetables (such as carrots, peas, and corn)
- 1/4 cup chopped fresh parsley
- Salt and pepper, to taste
- 1/4 cup grated parmesan cheese

Instructions:

1. Preheat oven to 375°F. Line a 9x13 inch baking dish with parchment paper or aluminum foil.

2. Cut off the tops of the tomatoes and scoop out the seeds and flesh with a spoon. Reserve the tops and place the hollowed-out tomatoes in the prepared baking dish.

3. In a medium saucepan, bring the quinoa and chicken or vegetable broth to a boil. Reduce heat and let simmer for 15-20 minutes, or until the liquid is fully absorbed and the quinoa is cooked.

4. In a large skillet, heat the olive oil over medium heat. Add the onion and cook until soft and translucent, about 5-7 minutes.

5. Add the garlic, mixed vegetables, and parsley to the skillet and cook for 5-7 minutes, or until the vegetables are tender.

6. Stir in the cooked quinoa and season with salt and pepper to taste.

7. Fill the hollowed-out tomatoes with the quinoa mixture, mounding it slightly on top.

8. Sprinkle the grated parmesan cheese over the top of the tomatoes.

9. Place the reserved tomato tops on top of the cheese.

10. Bake for 25-30 minutes, or until the tomatoes are tender and the cheese is melted and bubbly.

11. Serve hot and enjoy!

BEEF STROGANOFF

Ingredients:

- 1 lb sirloin steak, sliced into thin strips
- Salt and pepper, to taste
- 2 tablespoons olive oil
- 1 onion, diced
- 2 garlic cloves, minced
- 1 cup sliced mushrooms
- 1 tablespoon flour
- 1 cup beef broth
- 1 cup sour cream
- 1 lb egg noodles

Instructions:

1. Season the sliced sirloin steak with salt and pepper.

2. In a large skillet, heat the olive oil over medium heat. Add the onion and cook until soft and translucent, about 5-7 minutes.

3. Add the garlic and mushrooms to the skillet and cook for an additional 5-7 minutes, or until the mushrooms are tender.

4. Stir in the flour and cook for 1-2 minutes, or until the mixture has thickened slightly.

5. Gradually whisk in the beef broth and let simmer for 5-7 minutes, or until the sauce has thickened slightly.

6. Stir in the sour cream and let simmer for an additional 2-3 minutes, or until heated through.

7. In a large pot of boiling salted water, cook the egg noodles according to package instructions until al dente.

8. Drain the noodles and serve with the beef stroganoff sauce spooned over the top.

CHICKEN ENCHILADAS WITH GREEN SAUCE

Ingredients:

- 8 corn tortillas
- 2 cups cooked and shredded chicken
- 1 cup grated cheese
- 1 cup green enchilada sauce
- 1/4 cup chopped fresh cilantro

Instructions:

1. Preheat the oven to 350°F. Grease a 9x13 inch baking dish.

2. In a large bowl, mix together the cooked chicken, 1/2 cup of grated cheese, and 2 tablespoons of chopped cilantro.

3. Pour 1/4 cup of enchilada sauce into the bottom of the prepared baking dish.

4. Fill each tortilla with the chicken mixture, roll it up, and place it seam-side down in the baking dish.

5. Pour the remaining enchilada sauce over the top of the tortillas.

6. Sprinkle the remaining cheese on top.

7. Bake for 20-25 minutes or until the cheese is melted and the enchiladas are heated through.

8. Serve with chopped cilantro and extra sauce if desired.

BAKED ZITI WITH SPINACH AND MUSHROOMS

Ingredients:

- 1 pound ziti pasta
- 2 tablespoons olive oil
- 1 onion, diced
- 3 cloves garlic, minced
- 8 ounces mushrooms, sliced
- 5 cups fresh spinach
- 1 (24-ounce) jar marinara sauce
- 1 cup ricotta cheese
- 1 cup grated mozzarella cheese
- 1/4 cup grated parmesan cheese

Instructions:

1. Preheat the oven to 375°F. Grease a 9x13 inch baking dish.

2. Cook the ziti pasta according to package instructions until al dente. Drain and set aside.

3. In a large pan, heat the olive oil over medium heat. Add the onion and cook for 5 minutes or until softened.

4. Add the garlic, mushrooms, and spinach to the pan and cook for an additional 5 minutes or until the spinach has wilted.

5. In a large bowl, mix together the cooked ziti, marinara sauce, ricotta cheese, mozzarella cheese, and parmesan cheese.

6. Stir in the cooked vegetable mixture.

7. Pour the ziti mixture into the prepared baking dish.

8. Bake for 25-30 minutes or until the cheese is melted and bubbly.

9. Let cool for 5 minutes before serving.

FISH TACOS WITH AVOCADO CREMA

Ingredients:

- 1 pound white fish fillets (such as cod or tilapia)
- 1 teaspoon chili powder
- 1/2 teaspoon cumin
- 1/2 teaspoon paprika
- 1/4 teaspoon garlic powder
- 1/4 teaspoon salt
- 8 small flour tortillas
- 1 avocado, mashed
- 1/2 cup sour cream
- 1 lime, juiced
- 1/4 cup chopped fresh cilantro
- 1/2 cup shredded red cabbage

Instructions:

1. Preheat the oven to 400°F. Line a baking sheet with parchment paper.

2. In a small bowl, mix together the chili powder, cumin, paprika, garlic powder, and salt.

3. Rub the spice mixture onto both sides of the fish fillets.

4. Bake the fish for 10-12 minutes or until fully cooked and flaky.

5. In another small bowl, mix together the mashed avocado, sour cream, lime juice, and cilantro.

6. Warm the tortillas in the oven for a few minutes.

7. To assemble the tacos, place a piece of fish in each tortilla, top with the avocado crema, shredded cabbage, and extra cilantro if desired.

8. Serve immediately.

GREEK-STYLE STUFFED CHICKEN

Ingredients:

- 4 boneless, skinless chicken breasts
- 1 cup chopped baby spinach
- 1/2 cup crumbled feta cheese
- 1/4 cup chopped kalamata olives
- 1/4 cup chopped sun-dried tomatoes
- 2 tablespoons chopped fresh basil
- 1 tablespoon lemon juice
- 1/4 teaspoon salt
- 1/4 teaspoon black pepper
- 1 tablespoon olive oil

Instructions:

1. Preheat the oven to 400°F. Line a baking sheet with parchment paper.

2. Using a sharp knife, cut a pocket into the side of each chicken breast.

3. In a small bowl, mix together the spinach, feta cheese, olives, sun-dried tomatoes, basil, lemon juice, salt, and pepper.

4. Stuff each chicken breast with the mixture.

5. In a large pan, heat the olive oil over medium heat. Add the stuffed chicken breasts and cook for 2-3 minutes on each side or until lightly browned.

6. Transfer the chicken to the prepared baking sheet.

7. Bake for 20-25 minutes or until the chicken is fully cooked and the filling is heated through.

8. Serve with additional lemon wedges and chopped basil if desired.

GRILLED VEGETABLE KABOBS WITH QUINOA

Ingredients:

- 1 red bell pepper, cut into 1 inch pieces
- 1 yellow bell pepper, cut into 1 inch pieces
- 1 red onion, cut into 1 inch pieces
- 1 zucchini, cut into 1 inch pieces
- 1 yellow squash, cut into 1 inch pieces
- 1 pint cherry tomatoes
- 1/4 cup olive oil
- 1 teaspoon salt
- 1/2 teaspoon black pepper
- 1 teaspoon dried basil
- 1 teaspoon dried oregano
- 1 cup quinoa

- 2 cups water

Instructions:

1. Preheat a grill to medium-high heat.

2. In a large bowl, mix together the bell peppers, onion, zucchini, yellow squash, cherry tomatoes, olive oil, salt, pepper, basil, and oregano.

3. Thread the vegetables onto skewers, alternating between each type.

4. Grill the kabobs for 10-12 minutes or until the vegetables are tender and slightly charred.

5. In a medium saucepan, bring the quinoa and water to a boil. Reduce heat to low, cover, and simmer for 18-20 minutes or until the quinoa is fully cooked.

6. Serve the kabobs over a bed of cooked quinoa.

CHICKEN MARSALA

Ingredients:

- 4 boneless, skinless chicken breasts
- 1/2 teaspoon salt
- 1/2 teaspoon black pepper
- 1/2 cup all-purpose flour
- 2 tablespoons olive oil
- 8 ounces mushrooms, sliced
- 1 onion, diced
- 3 cloves garlic, minced
- 1 cup chicken broth
- 1/2 cup Marsala wine
- 2 tablespoons butter

- 2 tablespoons chopped fresh parsley

Instructions:

1. Season both sides of the chicken breasts with salt and pepper.

2. Place the flour in a shallow dish. Dredge each chicken breast in the flour, shaking off any excess.

3. In a large pan, heat the olive oil over medium heat. Add the chicken breasts and cook for 5-7 minutes on each side or until browned and fully cooked. Remove from the pan and set aside.

4. In the same pan, add the mushrooms, onion, and garlic. Cook for 5-7 minutes or until softened.

5. Add the chicken broth, Marsala wine, and butter to the pan. Stir to combine and bring to a simmer.

6. Return the chicken breasts to the pan and spoon the sauce over the top.

7. Serve with additional sauce and sprinkled with fresh parsley.

TOFU AND VEGETABLE STIR-FRY

Ingredients:

- 1 block firm tofu, drained and cubed
- 1 red bell pepper, sliced
- 1 yellow bell pepper, sliced
- 1 red onion, sliced
- 1 cup sliced mushrooms
- 1 tablespoon sesame oil

- 1/4 teaspoon salt
- 1/4 teaspoon black pepper
- 1 tablespoon soy sauce
- 1 tablespoon cornstarch
- 2 tablespoons water
- 1 tablespoon vegetable oil
- 1/4 cup chopped fresh cilantro

Instructions:

1. In a large pan, heat the sesame oil over medium heat. Add the tofu and cook for 5-7 minutes or until lightly browned. Remove from the pan and set aside.

2. In the same pan, add the red pepper, yellow pepper, red onion, and mushrooms. Cook for 5-7 minutes or until softened.

3. In a small bowl, whisk together the salt, pepper, soy sauce, cornstarch, and water.

4. Add the vegetable oil to the pan with the vegetables. Stir in the tofu and the cornstarch mixture.

5. Cook for an additional 2-3 minutes or until the sauce has thickened.

6. Serve with a sprinkle of chopped cilantro on top.

CHICKEN FAJITAS

Ingredients:

- 1 pound boneless, skinless chicken breasts, sliced into strips
- 1 red bell pepper, sliced
- 1 yellow bell pepper, sliced

- 1 red onion, sliced
- 2 tablespoons olive oil
- 1 teaspoon chili powder
- 1 teaspoon paprika
- 1/2 teaspoon cumin
- 1/2 teaspoon garlic powder
- 1/2 teaspoon salt
- 1/4 teaspoon black pepper
- 8 small flour tortillas

Instructions:

1. In a large bowl, mix together the chicken, red pepper, yellow pepper, red onion, olive oil, chili powder, paprika, cumin, garlic powder, salt, and pepper.

2. In a large pan, cook the chicken and vegetable mixture over medium heat for 10-12 minutes or until the chicken is fully cooked and the vegetables are tender.

3. Warm the tortillas in the oven or on a griddle.

4. Serve the chicken and vegetable mixture in the warm tortillas. Top with additional toppings of your choice such as cheese, salsa, and sour cream.

POT ROAST WITH CARROTS AND POTATOES

Ingredients:

- 3-4 pound beef roast
- 1 teaspoon salt
- 1/2 teaspoon black pepper
- 2 tablespoons olive oil
- 1 onion, diced
- 3 cloves garlic, minced

- 1 cup beef broth
- 1/2 cup red wine
- 2 teaspoons dried thyme
- 3 carrots, peeled and chopped
- 3 potatoes, peeled and chopped

Instructions:

1. Preheat the oven to 325°F.

2. Season the beef roast with salt and pepper.

3. In a large oven-safe pan, heat the olive oil over medium heat. Add the beef roast and brown on all sides for 5-7 minutes.

4. Add the onion and garlic to the pan and cook for 2-3 minutes or until softened.

5. Pour in the beef broth, red wine, and sprinkle with thyme. Stir to combine.

6. Add the carrots and potatoes to the pan, surrounding the beef roast.

7. Cover the pan with foil and transfer to the oven. Bake for 2-3 hours or until the beef is fully cooked and tender.

8. Serve the pot roast with the carrots and potatoes.

GRILLED FISH WITH HERB BUTTER

Ingredients:

- 4 fish fillets (such as salmon or tilapia)
- 1 tablespoon olive oil
- 1 teaspoon salt

- 1/2 teaspoon black pepper
- 1/4 cup butter, melted
- 1 tablespoon lemon juice
- 1 teaspoon dried basil
- 1 teaspoon dried thyme

Instructions:

1. Preheat a grill to medium-high heat.

2. Brush both sides of the fish fillets with olive oil and season with salt and pepper.

3. In a small bowl, mix together the melted butter, lemon juice, basil, and thyme.

4. Place the fish fillets on the grill and brush with the herb butter mixture.

5. Grill the fish for 5-7 minutes on each side or until fully cooked and flaky.

6. Serve with additional lemon wedges and chopped herbs if desired.

BAKED COD WITH TOMATOES AND OLIVES

Ingredients:

- 4 cod fillets
- 1 teaspoon salt
- 1/2 teaspoon black pepper
- 1 tablespoon olive oil
- 1 pint cherry tomatoes, halved
- 1/2 cup pitted kalamata olives
- 1 lemon, thinly sliced
- 1/4 cup chopped fresh parsley

Instructions:

1. Preheat the oven to 400°F. Line a baking sheet with parchment paper.

2. Season the cod fillets with salt and pepper.

3. In a large bowl, mix together the cherry tomatoes, olives, lemon slices, and parsley.

4. Arrange the cod fillets on the prepared baking sheet. Spoon the tomato and olive mixture over the top of the cod.

5. Drizzle with olive oil.

6. Bake for 15-20 minutes or until the cod is fully cooked and flaky.

7. Serve with additional lemon wedges and chopped parsley if desired.

LEMON HERB ROASTED CHICKEN

Ingredients:

- 1 whole chicken (3-4 pounds)
- 1 lemon, halved
- 2 tablespoons butter, melted
- 1 teaspoon salt
- 1/2 teaspoon black pepper
- 1 teaspoon dried basil
- 1 teaspoon dried thyme
- 1 teaspoon dried rosemary

Instructions:

1. Preheat the oven to 425°F. Line a baking sheet with parchment paper or foil.

2. Rinse and dry the chicken. Place the chicken on the prepared baking sheet.

3. Squeeze the lemon juice over the chicken.

4. In a small bowl, mix together the melted butter, salt, pepper, basil, thyme, and rosemary.

5. Use your hands to rub the butter mixture all over the chicken, making sure to get some of the mixture under the skin as well.

6. Place the lemon halves inside the cavity of the chicken.

7. Roast the chicken for 1 hour and 15 minutes to 1 hour and 30 minutes or until the internal temperature of the chicken reaches 165°F.

8. Let the chicken rest for 10 minutes before carving and serving.

MEATLOAF WITH MUSHROOM GRAVY

Ingredients:

- 1 1/2 pounds ground beef
- 1 egg, beaten
- 1/2 cup breadcrumbs
- 1/2 cup milk
- 1/2 onion, diced
- 3 cloves garlic, minced
- 1 teaspoon salt
- 1/2 teaspoon black pepper
- 1 tablespoon olive oil

- 8 ounces sliced mushrooms
- 1 cup beef broth
- 2 tablespoons cornstarch
- 2 tablespoons water

Instructions:

1. Preheat the oven to 375°F. Line a 9x5 inch loaf pan with parchment paper or foil.

2. In a large bowl, mix together the ground beef, egg, breadcrumbs, milk, onion, garlic, salt, and pepper.

3. Transfer the mixture to the prepared loaf pan and shape into a loaf.

4. Bake for 45-50 minutes or until the internal temperature of the meatloaf reaches 160°F.

5. In a large pan, heat the olive oil over medium heat. Add the mushrooms and cook for 5-7 minutes or until tender.

6. Add the beef broth to the pan and bring to a simmer.

7. In a small bowl, mix together the cornstarch and water to form a slurry.

8. Pour the slurry into the pan and stir until the gravy thickens, about 1-2 minutes.

9. Serve the meatloaf with the mushroom gravy.

VEGETABLE PAELLA

Ingredients:

- 2 tablespoons olive oil
- 1 onion, diced
- 3 cloves garlic, minced
- 1 red bell pepper, sliced
- 1 yellow bell pepper, sliced
- 1 cup arborio rice
- 1 can diced tomatoes
- 2 cups vegetable broth
- 1 teaspoon paprika
- 1/2 teaspoon saffron threads
- 1/2 teaspoon salt
- 1/4 teaspoon black pepper
- 1 cup frozen peas
- 1 cup sliced mushrooms

Instructions:

1. In a large pan, heat the olive oil over medium heat. Add the onion and garlic and cook for 2-3 minutes or until softened.

2. Add the red and yellow bell peppers to the pan and cook for another 2-3 minutes.

3. Add the rice to the pan and stir to combine. Cook for 1-2 minutes or until the rice is lightly toasted.

4. Pour in the diced tomatoes, vegetable broth, paprika, saffron, salt, and pepper. Stir to combine.

5. Bring the mixture to a simmer. Reduce heat to low, cover the pan, and let cook for 18-20 minutes or until the rice is fully cooked and the liquid has been absorbed.

6. Stir in the frozen peas and sliced mushrooms. Cook for another 2-3 minutes or until the vegetables are tender.

7. Serve the vegetable paella hot.

CHICKEN POT PIE

Ingredients:

- 2 tablespoons butter
- 1 onion, diced
- 3 cloves garlic, minced
- 2 carrots, peeled and chopped
- 2 stalks celery, chopped
- 1 cup frozen peas
- 1 cup frozen corn
- 2 tablespoons flour
- 2 cups chicken broth
- 1 cup milk
- 1 teaspoon dried thyme
- 1/2 teaspoon salt
- 1/4 teaspoon black pepper
- 2 cups cooked and shredded chicken
- 2 refrigerated pie crusts

Instructions:

1. Preheat the oven to 425°F. Line a 9-inch pie dish with one of the pie crusts.

2. In a large pan, heat the butter over medium heat. Add the onion, garlic, carrots, and celery and cook for 5-7 minutes or until softened.

3. Stir in the frozen peas and corn. Cook for another 2-3 minutes.

4. Sprinkle the flour over the vegetable mixture and stir to combine. Cook for 1-2 minutes.

5. Pour in the chicken broth and milk. Stir to combine and bring to a simmer.

6. Add the thyme, salt, and pepper to the mixture. Stir to combine.

7. Stir in the cooked and shredded chicken.

8. Pour the mixture into the prepared pie dish. Top with the second pie crust, crimping the edges to seal.

9. Cut a few slits in the top of the crust to allow steam to escape.

10. Bake for 25-30 minutes or until the crust is golden brown and the filling is hot and bubbly.

11. Serve the chicken pot pie hot.

SPINACH AND MUSHROOM FRITTATA

Ingredients:

- 1 tablespoon olive oil
- 1 onion, diced
- 8 ounces sliced mushrooms
- 5 eggs
- 1/2 cup milk
- 1/2 teaspoon salt
- 1/4 teaspoon black pepper
- 2 cups fresh spinach
- 1/2 cup shredded cheddar cheese

Instructions:

1. Preheat the oven to 400°F.

2. In a large oven-safe pan, heat the olive oil over medium heat. Add the onion and mushrooms and cook for 5-7 minutes or until softened.

3. In a large bowl, whisk together the eggs, milk, salt, and pepper.

4. Stir in the cooked onion and mushroom mixture and the fresh spinach.

5. Pour the egg mixture into the pan and sprinkle the cheddar cheese over the top.

6. Place the pan in the oven and bake for 15-20 minutes or until the frittata is fully cooked and the cheese is melted.

7. Serve the spinach and mushroom frittata hot.

SESAME-CRUSTED TUNA WITH SOY-GINGER GLAZE

Ingredients:

- 4 tuna steaks
- 1/2 cup sesame seeds
- 1/4 cup soy sauce
- 2 tablespoons honey
- 1 tablespoon freshly grated ginger
- 1 clove garlic, minced
- 1 teaspoon sesame oil
- 1/4 teaspoon red pepper flakes

Instructions:

1. Preheat the oven to 400°F. Line a baking sheet with parchment paper or foil.

2. Place the sesame seeds on a plate. Dip each tuna steak into the sesame seeds, pressing the seeds into the fish to coat.

3. Place the coated tuna steaks on the prepared baking sheet.

4. In a small bowl, whisk together the soy sauce, honey, ginger, garlic, sesame oil, and red pepper flakes.

5. Brush the soy-ginger mixture over the top of each tuna steak.

6. Bake the tuna steaks for 10-12 minutes or until they are just cooked through.

7. Serve the sesame-crusted tuna hot with the remaining soy-ginger glaze on the side.

PESTO PASTA WITH SUN-DRIED TOMATOES AND ARTICHOKES

Ingredients:

- 1 pound spaghetti
- 1/2 cup basil pesto
- 1/2 cup sun-dried tomatoes, chopped
- 1 can artichoke hearts, drained and chopped
- 1/2 cup grated parmesan cheese

Instructions:

1. Cook the spaghetti according to the package instructions. Drain and set aside.

2. In a large bowl, mix together the cooked spaghetti, basil pesto, sun-dried tomatoes, and chopped artichoke hearts.

3. Stir in the grated parmesan cheese.

4. Serve the pesto pasta hot.

VEGETABLE STIR-FRY WITH BROWN RICE

Ingredients:

- 2 tablespoons vegetable oil
- 1 onion, diced
- 3 cloves garlic, minced
- 1 red bell pepper, sliced
- 1 yellow bell pepper, sliced
- 1 cup sliced mushrooms
- 1 cup broccoli florets
- 1 cup sliced carrots
- 1 cup snow peas
- 2 tablespoons soy sauce
- 2 tablespoons hoisin sauce
- 1 teaspoon cornstarch
- 2 cups cooked brown rice

Instructions:

1. In a large wok or pan, heat the vegetable oil over high heat. Add the onion and garlic and cook for 2-3 minutes or until softened.

2. Add the red and yellow bell peppers, mushrooms, broccoli, carrots, and snow peas to the pan. Cook for 5-7 minutes or until the vegetables are tender.

3. In a small bowl, whisk together the soy sauce, hoisin sauce, and cornstarch.

4. Pour the sauce mixture into the pan and stir to combine. Cook for another 1-2 minutes or until the sauce has thickened.

5. Serve the vegetable stir-fry over a bed of cooked brown rice.

SHRIMP SCAMPI WITH LINGUINE

Ingredients:

- 1 pound linguine
- 2 tablespoons butter
- 3 cloves garlic, minced
- 1 pound raw shrimp, peeled and deveined
- 1/2 cup white wine
- 1/2 lemon, juiced
- 1/4 teaspoon red pepper flakes
- 1/2 teaspoon salt
- 1/4 teaspoon black pepper
- 1/4 cup chopped fresh parsley

Instructions:

1. Cook the linguine according to the package instructions. Drain and set aside.

2. In a large pan, heat the butter over medium heat. Add the garlic and cook for 1-2 minutes or until fragrant.

3. Add the shrimp to the pan and cook for 2-3 minutes or until pink and fully cooked.

4. Pour in the white wine and lemon juice. Stir to combine.

5. Add the red pepper flakes, salt, and pepper to the pan. Stir to combine.

6. Stir in the cooked linguine.

7. Serve the shrimp scampi hot, sprinkled with chopped fresh parsley.

BEEF AND BROCCOLI STIR-FRY

Ingredients:

- 1 pound flank steak, sliced into thin strips
- 2 tablespoons vegetable oil
- 1 onion, diced
- 3 cloves garlic, minced
- 2 cups broccoli florets
- 1/2 cup beef broth
- 2 tablespoons soy sauce
- 1 tablespoon cornstarch
- 1 teaspoon brown sugar
- 1/4 teaspoon red pepper flakes

Instructions:

1. In a large wok or pan, heat the vegetable oil over high heat. Add the onion and garlic and cook for 2-3 minutes or until softened.

2. Add the sliced flank steak to the pan and cook for 3-4 minutes or until browned.

3. Add the broccoli florets to the pan and cook for 2-3 minutes or until tender.

4. In a small bowl, whisk together the beef broth, soy sauce, cornstarch, brown sugar, and red pepper flakes.

5. Pour the sauce mixture into the pan and stir to combine. Cook for another 1-2 minutes or until the sauce has thickened.

6. Serve the beef and broccoli stir-fry hot.

CHICKEN AND VEGETABLE KEBABS

Ingredients:

- 1 pound boneless, skinless chicken breasts, cut into 1-inch pieces
- 1 red bell pepper, cut into 1-inch pieces
- 1 yellow bell pepper, cut into 1-inch pieces
- 1 onion, cut into 1-inch pieces
- 8 ounces button mushrooms
- 2 tablespoons olive oil
- 1 teaspoon dried basil
- 1/2 teaspoon salt
- 1/4 teaspoon black pepper

Instructions:

1. Preheat the grill to medium-high heat.

2. On metal or wooden skewers, alternate the chicken pieces, red and yellow bell peppers, onion, and mushrooms.

3. In a small bowl, whisk together the olive oil, basil, salt, and pepper.

4. Brush the olive oil mixture over the kebabs.

5. Place the kebabs on the grill and cook for 10-12 minutes or until the chicken is fully cooked and the vegetables are tender, turning occasionally.

6. Serve the chicken and vegetable kebabs hot.

PENNE WITH ROASTED VEGETABLES AND GOAT CHEESE

Ingredients:

- 1 pound penne pasta
- 1 zucchini, sliced
- 1 yellow squash, sliced
- 1 red bell pepper, sliced
- 1 yellow bell pepper, sliced
- 1 red onion, sliced
- 2 tablespoons olive oil
- 1 teaspoon dried basil
- 1/2 teaspoon salt
- 1/4 teaspoon black pepper
- 1/2 cup crumbled goat cheese

Instructions:

1. Preheat the oven to 400°F. Line a baking sheet with parchment paper or foil.

2. Cook the penne pasta according to the package instructions. Drain and set aside.

3. On the prepared baking sheet, place the sliced zucchini, yellow squash, red and yellow bell peppers, and red onion.

4. Drizzle the vegetables with olive oil and sprinkle with basil, salt, and pepper. Toss to coat.

5. Roast the vegetables in the oven for 20-25 minutes or until tender and lightly browned.

6. In a large bowl, mix together the cooked penne pasta, roasted vegetables, and crumbled goat cheese.

7. Serve the penne with roasted vegetables and goat cheese hot.

SEARED SCALLOPS WITH LEMON-GARLIC SAUCE

Ingredients:

- 1 pound sea scallops
- 2 tablespoons butter
- 3 cloves garlic, minced
- 1/2 cup chicken broth
- 1/2 lemon, juiced
- 1/4 teaspoon salt
- 1/4 teaspoon black pepper
- 1/4 cup chopped fresh parsley

Instructions:

1. In a large pan, heat the butter over medium heat. Add the garlic and cook for 1-2 minutes or until fragrant.

2. Pat the scallops dry with paper towels. Add the scallops to the pan and cook for 2-3 minutes on each side or until golden brown and fully cooked.

3. Remove the scallops from the pan and set aside.

4. Add the chicken broth, lemon juice, salt, and pepper to the pan. Stir to combine.

5. Return the scallops to the pan and spoon the lemon-garlic sauce over the top.

6. Serve the seared scallops hot, sprinkled with chopped fresh parsley.

CAULIFLOWER AND CHICKPEA CURRY

Ingredients:

- 2 tablespoons vegetable oil
- 1 onion, diced
- 3 cloves garlic, minced
- 1 teaspoon ginger, grated
- 2 teaspoons curry powder
- 1 teaspoon ground cumin
- 1/2 teaspoon ground coriander
- 1/2 teaspoon ground turmeric
- 1 can chickpeas, drained and rinsed
- 1 head cauliflower, chopped into florets
- 1 can diced tomatoes
- 1 cup chicken or vegetable broth
- 1/2 teaspoon salt
- 1/4 teaspoon black pepper
- 1/4 cup chopped fresh cilantro

Instructions:

1. In a large pot or Dutch oven, heat the vegetable oil over medium heat. Add the onion and garlic and cook for 2-3 minutes or until softened.

2. Add the ginger, curry powder, cumin, coriander, and turmeric to the pot and cook for 1-2 minutes or until fragrant.

3. Add the chickpeas, cauliflower, diced tomatoes, chicken or vegetable broth, salt, and pepper to the pot. Stir to combine.

4. Bring the curry to a simmer and cook for 20-25 minutes or until the cauliflower is tender.

5. Serve the cauliflower and chickpea curry hot, topped with chopped fresh cilantro.

SIDE DISHES

GARLIC MASHED POTATOES

Ingredients:

- 4 medium potatoes, peeled and chopped
- 3 cloves of garlic, minced
- 2 tablespoons of butter
- 1/2 cup of milk
- Salt and pepper to taste

Instructions:

1. Boil the chopped potatoes in a pot of salted water until they are soft. Drain the water and set aside.

2. In a separate pan, melt the butter over medium heat and add the minced garlic. Cook for about 2 minutes or until fragrant.

3. Mash the boiled potatoes in a large bowl and add the garlic butter mixture. Mix well.

4. Gradually add the milk while continuing to mash the potatoes until they reach a smooth and creamy consistency.

5. Season with salt and pepper to taste and serve hot.

ROASTED BRUSSELS SPROUTS WITH BALSAMIC GLAZE

Ingredients:

- 1 pound of Brussels sprouts, trimmed and halved
- 2 tablespoons of olive oil
- Salt and pepper to taste
- 1/4 cup of balsamic vinegar
- 2 tablespoons of honey

Instructions:

1. Preheat the oven to 400°F.

2. In a large bowl, toss the Brussels sprouts with olive oil, salt, and pepper until evenly coated.

3. Spread the Brussels sprouts on a baking sheet in a single layer and bake for 25-30 minutes or until tender and golden brown.

4. In a small saucepan, combine the balsamic vinegar and honey. Cook over medium heat, stirring constantly, until the mixture has reduced by half and thickened into a glaze.

5. Remove the Brussels sprouts from the oven and drizzle the balsamic glaze over them. Serve immediately.

SAUTÉED GREEN BEANS WITH ALMONDS

Ingredients:

- 1 pound of green beans, trimmed
- 2 tablespoons of olive oil
- 1/2 cup of sliced almonds

- 2 cloves of garlic, minced
- Salt and pepper to taste

Instructions:

1. Heat the olive oil in a large skillet over medium heat.

2. Add the sliced almonds and cook for 2-3 minutes or until golden brown. Remove from the skillet and set aside.

3. In the same skillet, add the minced garlic and cook for 1 minute or until fragrant.

4. Add the green beans to the skillet and cook, stirring occasionally, for 5-7 minutes or until tender.

5. Season with salt and pepper to taste and sprinkle the roasted almonds over the green beans before serving.

HERB-ROASTED CARROTS

Ingredients:

- 1 pound of carrots, peeled and chopped
- 2 tablespoons of olive oil
- 1 teaspoon of dried thyme
- 1 teaspoon of dried rosemary
- Salt and pepper to taste

Instructions:

1. Preheat the oven to 400°F.

2. In a large bowl, toss the chopped carrots with olive oil, dried thyme, dried rosemary, salt, and pepper until evenly coated.

3. Spread the carrots on a baking sheet in a single layer and bake for 25-30 minutes or until tender and golden brown.

4. Serve hot and enjoy the delicious herb flavor of the roasted carrots.

QUINOA AND VEGETABLE PILAF

Ingredients:

- 1 cup of quinoa, rinsed
- 2 cups of water
- 1 tablespoon of olive oil
- 1 onion, diced
- 1 red bell pepper, diced
- 1 cup of diced vegetables of your choice (such as carrots, zucchini, or mushrooms)
- Salt and pepper to taste

Instructions:

1. In a medium saucepan, bring the quinoa and water to a boil. Reduce the heat to low, cover, and simmer for 15-20 minutes or until the quinoa is tender and the water has been absorbed.

2. In a large skillet, heat the olive oil over medium heat.

3. Add the diced onion and cook for 2-3 minutes or until soft and translucent.

4. Add the diced red bell pepper and your choice of diced vegetables to the skillet and cook for 5-7 minutes or until tender.

5. Stir in the cooked quinoa and season with salt and pepper to taste. Serve hot as a flavorful and healthy side dish.

CREAMED SPINACH

Ingredients:

- 1 pound of fresh spinach, washed and chopped
- 2 tablespoons of butter
- 2 cloves of garlic, minced
- 2 tablespoons of all-purpose flour
- 1 cup of heavy cream
- Salt and pepper to taste
- 1/4 cup of grated Parmesan cheese (optional)

Instructions:

1. In a large pot, melt the butter over medium heat and add the minced garlic. Cook for about 2 minutes or until fragrant.

2. Stir in the flour and cook for 1-2 minutes or until the mixture turns a light brown color.

3. Gradually pour in the heavy cream while whisking constantly. Cook until the mixture has thickened and there are no lumps.

4. Add the chopped spinach to the pot and cook, stirring occasionally, for 5-7 minutes or until the spinach has wilted and the sauce has thickened further.

5. Season with salt and pepper to taste and sprinkle with grated Parmesan cheese, if desired. Serve hot as a creamy and delicious side dish.

GRILLED ASPARAGUS WITH LEMON ZEST

Ingredients:

- 1 pound of asparagus, trimmed
- 2 tablespoons of olive oil
- Zest of 1 lemon
- Salt and pepper to taste

Instructions:

1. Preheat a grill or grill pan to high heat.

2. In a large bowl, toss the asparagus with olive oil, lemon zest, salt, and pepper until evenly coated.

3. Place the asparagus on the grill or grill pan and cook for 5-7 minutes or until tender and lightly charred, turning occasionally.

4. Serve hot with a squeeze of lemon juice and enjoy the bright and flavorful taste of the grilled asparagus.

SWEET POTATO AND APPLE HASH

Ingredients:

- 2 medium sweet potatoes, peeled and diced
- 1 medium apple, peeled and diced
- 2 tablespoons of olive oil
- 1 teaspoon of cinnamon
- 1/4 teaspoon of nutmeg
- Salt and pepper to taste

Instructions:

1. In a large skillet, heat the olive oil over medium heat.

2. Add the diced sweet potatoes and cook for 5-7 minutes or until tender and lightly browned.

3. Add the diced apple to the skillet and cook for 2-3 minutes or until soft and slightly caramelized.

4. Stir in the cinnamon, nutmeg, salt, and pepper and cook for 1-2 minutes or until the flavors have combined.

5. Serve hot as a sweet and savory side dish, perfect for fall and winter meals.

BROWN RICE AND MUSHROOM RISOTTO

Ingredients:

- 1 cup of brown rice
- 2 cups of chicken or vegetable broth
- 1 tablespoon of olive oil
- 1 onion, diced
- 8 ounces of mushrooms, sliced
- 1/4 cup of white wine (optional)
- Salt and pepper to taste
- 1/4 cup of grated Parmesan cheese (optional)

Instructions:

1. In a medium saucepan, bring the brown rice and broth to a boil. Reduce the heat to low, cover, and simmer for 30-40 minutes or until the rice is tender and the liquid has been absorbed.

2. In a large skillet, heat the olive oil over medium heat.

3. Add the diced onion and cook for 2-3 minutes or until soft and translucent.

4. Add the sliced mushrooms to the skillet and cook for 5-7 minutes or until tender and lightly browned.

5. If using, add the white wine to the skillet and cook for 2-3 minutes or until it has reduced by half.

6. Stir in the cooked brown rice and season with salt and pepper to taste.

7. Serve hot, sprinkled with grated Parmesan cheese, if desired, for a hearty and flavorful side dish.

PARMESAN POLENTA

Ingredients:

- 4 cups of water
- 1 cup of coarse cornmeal
- 2 tablespoons of butter
- 1/2 cup of grated Parmesan cheese
- Salt and pepper to taste

Instructions:

1. In a medium saucepan, bring the water to a boil.

2. Gradually pour in the coarse cornmeal while whisking constantly. Reduce the heat to low and continue to stir for 5-7 minutes or until the mixture has thickened and there are no lumps.

3. Stir in the butter, grated Parmesan cheese, salt, and pepper until the butter has melted and the cheese has melted and combined with the polenta.

4. Serve hot as a creamy and cheesy side dish, perfect for soaking up sauces and gravies.

SALADS

SPINACH AND STRAWBERRY SALAD WITH BALSAMIC VINAIGRETTE

Ingredients:

- 6 cups fresh spinach
- 1 cup strawberries, hulled and sliced
- 1/4 cup walnuts, chopped
- 1/4 cup crumbled goat cheese
- For the vinaigrette:
- 3 tablespoons balsamic vinegar
- 2 tablespoons extra-virgin olive oil
- 1 tablespoon honey
- 1 teaspoon Dijon mustard
- Salt and pepper, to taste

Instructions:

1. In a large bowl, combine the spinach, strawberries, walnuts, and goat cheese.

2. In a small bowl, whisk together the balsamic vinegar, olive oil, honey, and Dijon mustard. Season with salt and pepper to taste.

3. Drizzle the vinaigrette over the salad and toss to combine.

4. Serve immediately and enjoy!

GREEK SALAD WITH FETA AND OLIVES

Ingredients:

- 2 large tomatoes, chopped
- 1 English cucumber, chopped
- 1 red onion, sliced
- 1 green bell pepper, sliced
- 1 cup kalamata olives
- 1/2 cup crumbled feta cheese
- For the dressing:
- 3 tablespoons extra-virgin olive oil
- 2 tablespoons red wine vinegar
- 1 clove garlic, minced
- 1 teaspoon dried oregano
- Salt and pepper, to taste

Instructions:

1. In a large bowl, combine the tomatoes, cucumber, red onion, bell pepper, olives, and feta cheese.

2. In a small bowl, whisk together the olive oil, red wine vinegar, garlic, and oregano. Season with salt and pepper to taste.

3. Drizzle the dressing over the salad and toss to combine.

4. Serve immediately and enjoy!

KALE AND QUINOA SALAD WITH LEMON-TAHINI DRESSING

Ingredients:

- 4 cups chopped kale
- 1 cup cooked quinoa
- 1/2 cup cherry tomatoes, halved
- 1/4 cup diced red onion
- 1/4 cup crumbled feta cheese
- For the dressing:
- 3 tablespoons tahini
- 2 tablespoons lemon juice
- 2 tablespoons water
- 1 clove garlic, minced
- Salt and pepper, to taste

Instructions:

1. In a large bowl, combine the kale, quinoa, cherry tomatoes, red onion, and feta cheese.

2. In a small bowl, whisk together the tahini, lemon juice, water, and garlic. Season with salt and pepper to taste.

3. Drizzle the dressing over the salad and toss to combine.

4. Serve immediately and enjoy!

MIXED GREENS WITH GRILLED CHICKEN, CRANBERRIES, AND GOAT CHEESE

Ingredients:

- 6 cups mixed greens
- 2 grilled chicken breasts, sliced

- 1/2 cup dried cranberries
- 1/4 cup crumbled goat cheese
- 1/4 cup chopped pecans
- For the dressing:
- 3 tablespoons balsamic vinaigrette

Instructions:

1. In a large bowl, combine the mixed greens, grilled chicken, cranberries, goat cheese, and pecans.

2. Drizzle the balsamic vinaigrette over the salad and toss to combine.

3. Serve immediately and enjoy!

CLASSIC CAESAR SALAD

Ingredients:

- 6 cups chopped romaine lettuce
- 1/2 cup croutons
- 1/2 cup grated parmesan cheese
- For the dressing:
- 3 tablespoons mayonnaise
- 2 tablespoons lemon juice
- 2 tablespoons grated parmesan cheese
- 1 clove garlic, minced
- Salt and pepper, to taste

Instructions:

1. In a large bowl, combine the romaine lettuce, croutons, and parmesan cheese.

2. In a small bowl, whisk together the mayonnaise, lemon juice, parmesan cheese, and garlic. Season with salt and pepper to taste.

3. Drizzle the dressing over the salad and toss to combine.

4. Serve immediately and enjoy!

BEET AND GOAT CHEESE SALAD WITH WALNUTS

Ingredients:

- 4 cups mixed greens
- 2 roasted beets, sliced
- 1/4 cup crumbled goat cheese
- 1/4 cup chopped walnuts
- For the dressing:
- 3 tablespoons balsamic vinaigrette

Instructions:

1. In a large bowl, combine the mixed greens, roasted beets, goat cheese, and walnuts.

2. Drizzle the balsamic vinaigrette over the salad and toss to combine.

3. Serve immediately and enjoy!

ARUGULA, PEAR, AND BLUE CHEESE SALAD

Ingredients:

- 6 cups arugula
- 2 ripe pears, sliced
- 1/2 cup crumbled blue cheese
- For the dressing:
- 3 tablespoons balsamic vinaigrette

Instructions:

1. In a large bowl, combine the arugula, pears, and blue cheese.

2. Drizzle the balsamic vinaigrette over the salad and toss to combine.

3. Serve immediately and enjoy!

COBB SALAD WITH AVOCADO DRESSING

Ingredients:

- 6 cups mixed greens
- 2 grilled chicken breasts, sliced
- 2 hard-boiled eggs, chopped
- 1 avocado, diced
- 1/2 cup cherry tomatoes, halved
- 1/4 cup crumbled blue cheese
- For the dressing:
- 1 ripe avocado, peeled and pitted
- 3 tablespoons lemon juice
- 2 tablespoons extra-virgin olive oil
- Salt and pepper, to taste

Instructions:

1. In a large bowl, combine the mixed greens, grilled chicken, eggs, avocado, cherry tomatoes, and blue cheese.

2. In a blender, puree the avocado, lemon juice, olive oil, salt, and pepper until smooth.

3. Drizzle the dressing over the salad and toss to combine.

4. Serve immediately and enjoy!

ASIAN NOODLE SALAD WITH SESAME-SOY DRESSING

Ingredients:

- 4 cups cooked Asian noodles
- 1 red bell pepper, sliced
- 1 yellow bell pepper, sliced
- 1 cup shredded carrots
- 1/4 cup chopped cilantro
- For the dressing:
- 3 tablespoons soy sauce
- 2 tablespoons rice vinegar
- 2 tablespoons sesame oil
- 1 tablespoon honey
- 1 teaspoon grated ginger

Instructions:

1. In a large bowl, combine the noodles, bell peppers, carrots, and cilantro.

2. In a small bowl, whisk together the soy sauce, rice vinegar, sesame oil, honey, and ginger.

3. Drizzle the dressing over the salad and toss to combine.

4. Serve immediately and enjoy!

TOMATO, CUCUMBER, AND RED ONION SALAD WITH FETA

Ingredients:

- 2 large tomatoes, chopped
- 1 English cucumber, chopped
- 1 red onion, sliced
- 1/2 cup crumbled feta cheese
- For the dressing:
- 3 tablespoons red wine vinegar
- 2 tablespoons extra-virgin olive oil
- 1 clove garlic, minced
- 1 teaspoon dried oregano
- Salt and pepper, to taste

Instructions:

1. In a large bowl, combine the tomatoes, cucumber, red onion, and feta cheese.

2. In a small bowl, whisk together the red wine vinegar, olive oil, garlic, and oregano. Season with salt and pepper to taste.

3. Drizzle the dressing over the salad and toss to combine.

4. Serve immediately and enjoy!

SNACKS

VEGETABLE STICKS WITH HUMMUS

Ingredients:

- 1 carrot, peeled and cut into sticks
- 1 cucumber, cut into sticks
- 1 red bell pepper, cut into sticks
- 1/2 cup hummus

Instructions:

1. Wash and prepare the vegetables by cutting them into sticks.

2. Serve the vegetables on a plate with a small bowl of hummus for dipping.

GREEK YOGURT WITH HONEY AND NUTS

Ingredients:

- 1 cup Greek yogurt
- 1 tablespoon honey
- 1/4 cup chopped nuts (almonds, walnuts, or pecans)

Instructions:

1. In a bowl, mix the Greek yogurt and honey until well combined.

2. Top the yogurt with chopped nuts.

3. Serve immediately and enjoy!

COTTAGE CHEESE WITH FRESH FRUIT

Ingredients:

- 1 cup cottage cheese
- 1 cup fresh fruit (such as berries, melon, or peaches)

Instructions:

1. In a bowl, mix the cottage cheese and fresh fruit.

2. Serve immediately and enjoy!

RICE CAKES WITH ALMOND BUTTER AND BANANA

Ingredients:

- 2 rice cakes
- 2 tablespoons almond butter
- 1 banana, sliced

Instructions:

1. Spread a tablespoon of almond butter on each rice cake.

2. Top each rice cake with sliced bananas.

3. Serve immediately and enjoy!

WHOLE-GRAIN CRACKERS WITH CHEESE

Ingredients:

- 8 whole-grain crackers
- 4 ounces cheese (cheddar, Swiss, or your favorite variety)

Instructions:

1. Place 4 crackers on a plate and top each with a slice of cheese.

2. Place the remaining 4 crackers on top of the cheese to make 4 cheese sandwiches.

3. Serve immediately and enjoy!

APPLE SLICES WITH PEANUT BUTTER

Ingredients:

- 2 apples, sliced
- 2 tablespoons peanut butter

Instructions:

1. Slice the apples and arrange on a plate.

2. Spread a tablespoon of peanut butter on each slice of apple.

3. Serve immediately and enjoy!

ROASTED CHICKPEAS WITH SPICES

Ingredients:

- 1 can chickpeas, drained and rinsed
- 1 tablespoon olive oil
- 1 teaspoon salt
- 1 teaspoon paprika
- 1/2 teaspoon cumin

Instructions:

1. Preheat the oven to 400°F (200°C).

2. In a bowl, mix the chickpeas with olive oil, salt, paprika, and cumin.

3. Spread the chickpeas in a single layer on a baking sheet.

4. Bake for 20-25 minutes, until crispy and golden brown.

5. Serve immediately and enjoy!

TRAIL MIX WITH NUTS, SEEDS, AND DRIED FRUIT

Ingredients:

- 1/2 cup nuts (almonds, walnuts, or pecans)
- 1/2 cup seeds (sunflower or pumpkin seeds)
- 1/2 cup dried fruit (raisins, cranberries, or chopped dates)

Instructions:

1. In a bowl, mix the nuts, seeds, and dried fruit.

2. Serve in a small bowl or bag for snacking.

BAKED KALE CHIPS

Ingredients:

- 1 bunch kale, washed and dried
- 1 tablespoon olive oil
- 1 teaspoon salt

Instructions:

1. Preheat the oven to 350°F (175°C).

2. Remove the kale leaves from the stems and tear into bite-sized pieces.

3. In a bowl, mix the kale leaves with olive oil and salt.

4. Spread the kale in a single layer on a baking sheet.

5. Bake for 10-15 minutes, until crispy and golden brown.

6. Serve immediately and enjoy!

CHERRY TOMATOES AND MOZZARELLA SKEWERS

Ingredients:

- 1 pint cherry tomatoes
- 8 ounces mozzarella cheese, cut into small cubes
- 1/4 cup balsamic vinegar
- 2 tablespoons olive oil
- 1 teaspoon salt
- 1/2 teaspoon black pepper

Instructions:

1. Preheat the grill or broiler.

2. Skewer the cherry tomatoes and mozzarella cubes, alternating each.

3. In a bowl, mix the balsamic vinegar, olive oil, salt, and pepper.

4. Brush the skewers with the balsamic mixture.

5. Grill or broil for 5-7 minutes, until the cheese is melted and the tomatoes are slightly charred.

6. Serve immediately and enjoy!

DESSERTS

APPLE CRISP WITH OAT TOPPING

Ingredients:

- 4 medium apples, peeled and sliced
- 1/2 cup rolled oats
- 1/2 cup all-purpose flour
- 1/2 cup brown sugar
- 1/2 teaspoon ground cinnamon
- 1/2 cup unsalted butter, melted

Instructions:

1. Preheat oven to 375°F. Grease a 9-inch square baking dish.

2. Arrange the sliced apples in the prepared dish.

3. In a separate bowl, mix together the oats, flour, brown sugar, and cinnamon.

4. Stir in the melted butter until the mixture is crumbly.

5. Sprinkle the oat mixture over the apples in the baking dish.

6. Bake for 30-35 minutes, or until the top is golden brown and the apples are tender.

BAKED PEARS WITH CINNAMON AND HONEY

Ingredients:

- 4 ripe pears, peeled and cored
- 1/4 cup honey
- 1/2 teaspoon ground cinnamon
- 1/4 cup unsalted butter, melted

Instructions:

1. Preheat oven to 375°F. Grease a 9-inch square baking dish.

2. Arrange the pears in the prepared dish.

3. In a small bowl, mix together the honey, cinnamon, and melted butter.

4. Spoon the mixture over the pears in the baking dish.

5. Bake for 25-30 minutes, or until the pears are tender and the sauce is bubbly.

MIXED BERRY FRUIT SALAD

Ingredients:

- 2 cups mixed berries (strawberries, blueberries, raspberries, etc.)
- 2 tablespoons honey
- 1 teaspoon lemon juice

Instructions:

1. Rinse and dry the mixed berries.

2. In a small bowl, whisk together the honey and lemon juice.

3. Pour the mixture over the mixed berries in a large bowl.

4. Toss gently to combine.

5. Serve chilled as a healthy and refreshing dessert option for two seniors.

LEMON YOGURT CAKE

Ingredients:

- 1 1/2 cups all-purpose flour
- 1 teaspoon baking powder
- 1/2 teaspoon baking soda
- 1/4 teaspoon salt
- 1/2 cup sugar
- 1/2 cup plain yogurt
- 2 large eggs
- 1/2 teaspoon vanilla extract
- 1/2 teaspoon lemon zest
- 1/4 cup lemon juice

Instructions:

1. Preheat oven to 350°F. Grease a 9-inch round cake pan.

2. In a medium bowl, whisk together the flour, baking powder, baking soda, and salt.

3. In a large bowl, beat together the sugar, yogurt, eggs, vanilla extract, lemon zest, and lemon juice until well combined.

4. Gradually add the dry ingredients to the wet ingredients, mixing until just combined.

5. Pour the batter into the prepared cake pan.

6. Bake for 25-30 minutes, or until a toothpick inserted into the center of the cake comes out clean.

DARK CHOCOLATE AND ALMOND BARK

Ingredients:

- 1 cup dark chocolate chips
- 1/2 cup whole almonds

Instructions:

1. Line a large baking sheet with parchment paper.

2. In a double boiler or a heatproof bowl set over a pot of simmering water, melt the chocolate chips until smooth.

3. Stir in the almonds into the melted chocolate.

4. Pour the chocolate mixture onto the prepared baking sheet and spread it into a thin, even layer.

5. Let the chocolate bark cool and harden at room temperature for 30 minutes or in the refrigerator for 10 minutes.

6. Once hardened, break the bark into pieces and serve as a rich and decadent dessert for two seniors.

PUMPKIN BREAD WITH WALNUTS

Ingredients:

- 1 1/2 cups all-purpose flour
- 1 teaspoon baking powder
- 1 teaspoon baking soda
- 1/2 teaspoon salt
- 1 teaspoon ground cinnamon
- 1/2 teaspoon ground nutmeg
- 1/2 teaspoon ground ginger
- 1/2 cup granulated sugar
- 1/2 cup brown sugar
- 1 cup pumpkin puree
- 2 large eggs
- 1/2 cup unsalted butter, melted
- 1/2 cup chopped walnuts

Instructions:

1. Preheat oven to 350°F. Grease a 9-inch loaf pan.

2. In a medium bowl, whisk together the flour, baking powder, baking soda, salt, cinnamon, nutmeg, and ginger.

3. In a large bowl, beat together the granulated sugar, brown sugar, pumpkin puree, eggs, and melted butter until well combined.

4. Gradually add the dry ingredients to the wet ingredients, mixing until just combined.

5. Stir in the chopped walnuts.

6. Pour the batter into the prepared loaf pan.

7. Bake for 50-60 minutes, or until a toothpick inserted into the center of the bread comes out clean.

RICE PUDDING WITH RAISINS AND CINNAMON

Ingredients:

- 1 cup short-grain white rice
- 2 cups water
- 1/2 teaspoon salt
- 2 cups whole milk
- 1/2 cup sugar
- 1 teaspoon ground cinnamon
- 1/2 cup raisins

Instructions:

1. In a medium saucepan, combine the rice, water, and salt. Bring to a boil over high heat.

2. Reduce heat to low, cover, and simmer for 18-20 minutes, or until the rice is tender and the water is absorbed.

3. Stir in the milk, sugar, and cinnamon into the cooked rice.

4. Increase heat to medium and cook, stirring frequently, for 15-20 minutes, or until the mixture thickens.

5. Stir in the raisins.

6. Serve warm or chilled as a comforting and satisfying dessert for two seniors.

FRESH FRUIT PARFAIT WITH VANILLA YOGURT

Ingredients:

- 2 cups mixed fresh fruit (strawberries, blueberries, raspberries, etc.)
- 1 cup plain vanilla yogurt
- 2 tablespoons honey

Instructions:

1. Rinse and dry the mixed fruit.

2. In a small bowl, mix together the yogurt and honey until well combined.

3. In two tall glasses or parfait cups, layer the fruit, yogurt mixture, and repeat until all ingredients are used.

4. Serve chilled as a healthy and refreshing dessert option for two seniors.

CARROT CAKE WITH CREAM CHEESE FROSTING

Ingredients:

- 1 1/2 cups all-purpose flour
- 1 teaspoon baking powder
- 1 teaspoon baking soda
- 1/2 teaspoon salt
- 1 teaspoon ground cinnamon
- 1/2 teaspoon ground nutmeg
- 1/2 cup granulated sugar
- 1/2 cup brown sugar
- 1 cup grated carrots

- 2 large eggs
- 1/2 cup unsalted butter, melted

Cream Cheese Frosting:

- 4 oz cream cheese, softened
- 1/4 cup unsalted butter, softened
- 2 cups powdered sugar
- 1 teaspoon vanilla extract

Instructions:

1. Preheat oven to 350°F. Grease a 9-inch round cake pan.

2. In a medium bowl, whisk together the flour, baking powder, baking soda, salt, cinnamon, and nutmeg.

3. In a large bowl, beat together the granulated sugar, brown sugar, grated carrots, eggs, and melted butter until well combined.

4. Gradually add the dry ingredients to the wet ingredients, mixing until just combined.

5. Pour the batter into the prepared cake pan.

6. Bake for 25-30 minutes, or until a toothpick inserted into the center of the cake comes out clean.

7. To make the frosting, in a large bowl, beat together the cream cheese, butter, powdered sugar, and vanilla extract until light and fluffy.

8. Once the cake has cooled, spread the frosting evenly over the top of the cake.

CHOCOLATE-DIPPED STRAWBERRIES

Ingredients:

- 1 cup dark chocolate chips
- 1 pint fresh strawberries, washed and dried

Instructions:

1. Line a large baking sheet with parchment paper.

2. In a double boiler or a heatproof bowl set over a pot of simmering water, melt the chocolate chips until smooth.

3. Dip each strawberry into the melted chocolate, using a toothpick or fork to hold it, and place on the prepared baking sheet.

4. Repeat with the remaining strawberries and chocolate.

5. Let the chocolate-dipped strawberries cool and harden at room temperature for 30 minutes or in the refrigerator for 10 minutes.

6. Serve as a sweet and simple dessert option for two seniors.

BLUEBERRY MUFFINS WITH STREUSEL TOPPING

Ingredients:

- 1 1/2 cups all-purpose flour
- 1 teaspoon baking powder
- 1/2 teaspoon baking soda
- 1/4 teaspoon salt
- 1/2 cup granulated sugar

- 1 large egg
- 1/2 cup plain yogurt
- 1/2 cup unsalted butter, melted
- 1 cup fresh blueberries

Streusel Topping:

- 1/4 cup all-purpose flour
- 1/4 cup brown sugar
- 1/4 teaspoon ground cinnamon
- 2 tablespoons unsalted butter, softened

Instructions:

1. Preheat oven to 375°F. Line a 12-cup muffin tin with muffin liners or grease with cooking spray.

2. In a medium bowl, whisk together the flour, baking powder, baking soda, and salt.

3. In a large bowl, beat together the sugar, egg, yogurt, and melted butter until well combined.

4. Gradually add the dry ingredients to the wet ingredients, mixing until just combined.

5. Fold in the blueberries.

6. To make the streusel topping, in a small bowl, mix together the flour, brown sugar, cinnamon, and softened butter until crumbly.

7. Fill each muffin cup about 2/3 full with the batter.

8. Sprinkle the streusel topping evenly over the batter in each muffin cup.

9. Bake for 18-20 minutes, or until a toothpick inserted into the center of a muffin comes out clean.

COCONUT MACAROONS

Ingredients:

- 3 cups shredded coconut
- 1/2 cup granulated sugar
- 4 large egg whites
- 1/4 teaspoon salt
- 1 teaspoon vanilla extract

Instructions:

1. Preheat oven to 325°F. Line a large baking sheet with parchment paper.

2. In a large bowl, mix together the coconut, sugar, egg whites, salt, and vanilla extract until well combined.

3. Using a cookie scoop or a tablespoon, drop the mixture onto the prepared baking sheet, spacing them about 2 inches apart.

4. Bake for 18-20 minutes, or until the edges are lightly golden.

5. Let the macaroons cool completely on the baking sheet.

6. Serve as a sweet and chewy dessert for two seniors.

CHOCOLATE CHIP OATMEAL COOKIES

Ingredients:

- 1 1/2 cups all-purpose flour

- 1 teaspoon baking powder
- 1/2 teaspoon baking soda
- 1/4 teaspoon salt
- 1/2 cup unsalted butter, softened
- 1/2 cup granulated sugar
- 1/2 cup brown sugar
- 1 large egg
- 1 teaspoon vanilla extract
- 1 1/2 cups rolled oats
- 1 cup semisweet chocolate chips

Instructions:

1. Preheat oven to 375°F. Line a large baking sheet with parchment paper.

2. In a medium bowl, whisk together the flour, baking powder, baking soda, and salt.

3. In a large bowl, beat together the butter, granulated sugar, brown sugar, egg, and vanilla extract until well combined.

4. Gradually add the dry ingredients to the wet ingredients, mixing until just combined.

5. Stir in the oats and chocolate chips.

6. Using a cookie scoop or a tablespoon, drop the mixture onto the prepared baking sheet, spacing them about 2 inches apart.

7. Bake for 12-14 minutes, or until the edges are lightly golden.

8. Let the cookies cool completely on the baking sheet.

BANANA BREAD WITH CHOCOLATE CHIPS

Ingredients:

- 1 1/2 cups all-purpose flour
- 1 teaspoon baking powder
- 1/2 teaspoon baking soda
- 1/4 teaspoon salt
- 1/2 cup unsalted butter, softened
- 1 cup granulated sugar
- 2 large eggs
- 3 ripe bananas, mashed
- 1 teaspoon vanilla extract
- 1 cup semisweet chocolate chips

Instructions:

1. Preheat oven to 350°F. Grease a 9x5 inch loaf pan.

2. In a medium bowl, whisk together the flour, baking powder, baking soda, and salt.

3. In a large bowl, beat together the butter and sugar until light and fluffy.

4. Beat in the eggs one at a time, then stir in the mashed bananas and vanilla extract.

5. Gradually add the dry ingredients to the wet ingredients, mixing until just combined.

6. Fold in the chocolate chips.

7. Pour the batter into the prepared loaf pan.

8. Bake for 55-60 minutes, or until a toothpick inserted into the center of the loaf comes out clean.

9. Let the banana bread cool completely in the pan.

POACHED PEACHES WITH
VANILLA ICE CREAM

Ingredients:

- 4 ripe peaches, pitted and halved
- 2 cups water
- 1 cup granulated sugar
- 1 teaspoon vanilla extract
- 1 pint vanilla ice cream

Instructions:

1. In a large saucepan, bring the water, sugar, and vanilla extract to a boil over medium heat.

2. Add the peach halves and reduce the heat to low. Simmer for 10-15 minutes, or until the peaches are soft and tender.

3. Remove the peaches from the syrup and let cool completely.

4. Serve the peaches with a scoop of vanilla ice cream on top as a sweet and simple dessert for two seniors.

RECIPES LIST

BREAKFASTS

SOUPS

STEWS

MAIN DISHES

SIDE DISHES

SALADS

SNACKS

DESSERTS

Printed in Great Britain
by Amazon

43470562R00076